D0564628

FOREWORD

My own life was dramatically influenced, or perhaps unknowingly altered, by a zoo, or more correctly, by a school with a zoo. Half-consciously aware of the adventure it would afford, I chose to attend the Millbrook School in Millbrook, New York, because it had a zoo. Certainly at the time I was unaware of how profound a decision it would prove to be for setting the future direction of my life. But even back then, within weeks after my arrival at the school, the zoo and its legendary biology teacher, Frank Trevor, had already begun to work their magic. I knew that I was indivertibly headed for a life as a biologist and conservationist. Indeed, I reveled in that educational experience, enjoying personal interaction with animals as diverse as a grey squirrel, named Singer for the sewing machine action of its teeth, and a cheetah, Caesar, who starred in Walt Disney's *The African Lion.* These lingering memories suggest the real delight I take now in making some prefatory remarks on behalf of this book about a zoo—most especially because it's the National Zoo.

It is particularly meaningful that the true origins of the National Zoo involved bringing American bison to graze and propagate on the Mall when their population had dwindled to alarmingly low numbers. Early on a few major zoos had been active in captive propagation, and by 1963 Gerald Durrell's Wildlife Preservation Trust had been established. But it is only quite recently that zoos as a whole have taken their conservation role seriously.

It should be abundantly clear, even without the grave peril to the biota posed by the greenhouse effect and global climate change, that landscapes are so modified and species so confined to isolated remnants of natural habitat that many will not be able to survive without the assist of captive propagation. That is no simple exercise; it involves field and laboratory science, painstaking record keeping, and fastidious care and concern. The complexity of the exercise plays itself out here in the pages of Jake Page's account. I am pleased to have played a bit part in it myself when in April 1980 the zoo registrar, Judith Block, turned over the first golden lion tamarins to me at Dulles International Airport to ride in a seat beside me (confirmed on a passenger ticket under Marmoset Lovejoy) to London and the Wildlife Preservation Trust on Jersey in the English Channel Islands. Never have I been accorded more VIP treatment—and appropriately so, given my diminutive fellow travelers.

At the zoo, as in any museum, much more goes on behind the scenes than the public sees, and this book shows the full variety of activities of the nation's zoo. For instance, presented here are the intensive training course in zoo biology and wildlife management provided for international students, the opportunities for field studies in faraway places, the analysis of crunching genetic statistics, or the investigation of behaviors that may relate to the origin of human speech. This volume demonstrates both the hard work and fun of it.

Despite these activities and their vital importance, zoos remain a primary—perhaps *the* primary— window on the sheer wonder and delight of the natural world and the by-and-large horrible things we are doing to it. This point is clearly something the National Zoo's imaginative current director, Michael Robinson, plans not to neglect. For example, the creation of the jewel-like Invertebrate Exhibit is just a beginning. There one can glimpse the lives of the spineless majority. Rarely have invertebrates been considered typical zoo inhabitants.

Building on the distinguished past, we can look forward to innovation in the zoo's public education role. Thank goodness we can, for there is no question that human society is on the brink of self-inflicted masochism through its adversarial stance against the natural world. Let us all wish our nation's zoo the greatest success in this effort to awaken the public to the challenge of the global environment. I hope in the future no one will have to comment, as one Millbrook schoolmate (who had never visited our school zoo) recently did: "When I first met you, why didn't you tell me I should try to save the world instead of playing football?"

Thomas E. Lovejoy
Assistant Secretary for
External Affairs
Smithsonian Institution

OUTWARD BOUND

On May 31, 1984, a delicate, long-fingered hand emerged from an open trapdoor on the top of a large wooden and wire mesh cage located in a ragged clearing in a desperately small remnant of Brazilian rain forest some sixty miles north of bustling, burgeoning Rio de Janeiro. In the silence, a sleek orange arm followed, then a fierce dark face surrounded by a reddish gold lionlike mane. Then, suddenly, out popped the entire brilliant animal, a nervous young male golden lion tamarin monkey, no bigger than a squirrel.

The male was followed by two others of its kind, the three animals perching skittishly atop the cage, called a *vivierro*, a jerry-built temporary home. They began darting back and forth across the top, in and out of the cage, and presently the adventurous male reached out and climbed adroitly onto a nearby branch. For the hushed group of American and Brazilian scientists watching from the edge of the clearing, it was a moment of almost feverish excitement and jubilation.

Science, we are told, is a dispassionate affair. At its core are hard facts, coolly collected and assessed and placed in a rational framework of hypothesis. Yet when this one monkey, known to the scientists as "number nine" and weighing scarcely more than a pound and a half, climbed out of its latest human-made home and leapt into the dense shrubbery beneath the canopy of the rain forest, it was a giant step for this species—and also in a real sense for humankind. Perhaps no one felt the powerful symbolism of this simple act more keenly than the handful of scientists present.

Golden lion tamarins once ranged over millions of hectares of continuous lowland forest along the Atlantic coast of Brazil. Logging, clear-cutting for cattle ranching and agriculture, and most recently, Rio de Janeiro's urban sprawl have eliminated most of this habitat. What little remains exists in small, fragmented islands in a sea of development. Even the Poço das Antas Reserve, a protected area, is bisected by a railroad. With the loss of habitat, golden lion tamarin numbers dropped precipitously to fewer than two hundred in the 1970s. At the same time the already small zoo population of tamarins was also declining. Led by National Zoo scientists, an intensive research and captive breeding program was begun to reverse these alarming trends. So successful was this program that in 1984 captive-bred tamarins began to be reintroduced in Brazil.

Back in the 1960s, little was known about golden lion tamarins, one of about twenty species of marmosets and tamarins known to South America. What was known was sobering. There was, first of all, a price on them. Because of their beauty and their active behavior, they made entertaining if fragile pets and zoo exhibits. Historically, groups of this creature had inhabited the damper, marshier areas of the lower montane rain forests, ranging from the site of the city of Rio de Janeiro northeast some six hundred kilometers along Brazil's Atlantic coast. By the late 1960s, the city and its satellite communities had taken over much of the tamarins' former habitat. All commercially valuable timber had been extracted and much of the remaining forest had been razed and burned, with the land put to use for catch-as-catch-can agriculture and pasture. Where rain forest had once rimmed the margin of land and sea, beach resort communities were snaking northeast along the coast. Caught in this pincer movement, most of the tamarins' habitat was lost. Some nine hundred square kilometers, according to a contemporary estimate, were all that was left and this was held exclusively in private hands. None of it was "forest primeval"; instead, there were discontinuous fragments, all in one stage or another of secondary succession. Only two percent of the original Atlantic lowland tropical rain forest survived. Few Brazilians had ever seen a golden lion tamarin; fewer still seemed to be alarmed at their possible demise.

Only one hundred of these vivid and lively creatures were thought to be scattered in the world's zoos at the time. Many had died in transit. In captivity disease was often lethal. Reproduction was uncommon and many of those infants born died of rickets. Adults occasionally died of herpes, respiratory ailments, gastrointestinal disease, or measles. Away from their native habitat, they often lost their vivid red-gold hue, their coats becoming pale and yellow. There was worldwide silence about these tamarins, the soundless dirge of approaching extinction. Even the Red Data Book, the publication of the International Union for the Conservation of Nature and Natural Resources (IUCN) that authoritatively catalogues the planet's rare and endangered species, had nothing to report about *Leontopithecus rosalia*.

The silence was effectively broken in October 1968 at a conference on Brazilian conservation problems. This was a time when, in the United States, the natural environment was only just becoming a widespread concern among the citizenry at large, and few people had ever heard of the emerging branch of biology called ecology. While the likes of Rachel Carson's *Silent Spring* and the lawsuits brought by the Sierra Club were rekindling a long American tradition of conservation, in Brazil the natural environment was, for the vast bulk of people and institutions, a fearsome frontier to be subdued as quickly as possible.

In those days, on the staff of the zoo in Rio de Janeiro, a man named Adelmar F. Coimbra-Filho was one of the few Brazilian biologists who had kept lion tamarins in captivity and attempted to study them in the wild. He had spent many days looking for glimpses of reddish gold in the few forest remnants near the São João River and had concluded that no more than six hundred golden lion tamarins existed in the wild.

One of the early speakers at the symposium, Coimbra urgently proposed that a reserve be established for these creatures and explained that unless both deforestation and trapping were halted, it was curtains for the golden lion tamarin.

The IUCN promptly added the tamarin to the Red Data Book and, in hopes of drying up the market for wild-caught specimens, urged zoos and other collectors around the world to stop buying the species. The Brazilian government banned export, reputable animal dealers eliminated the species from their price lists, and the American Association of Zoological Parks and Aquariums, among other zoo federations, agreed to stop importing the animals.

It should be pointed out, by the way, that there was at this time a considerable component of competitiveness among zoos. Thanks to Coimbra's passion, however, the golden lion tamarin had begun its seizure of the imagination, and it can be said with fairness that this little animal played an important early role in the still-growing revolution in zoological collections.

Having agreed not to mine wild populations for their exhibits, zoos were now thrown back on their own resources if the golden lion tamarin was to survive for very long as a zoo attraction, much less as a wild species. And those resources were severely impoverished. A new organization, the Wild Animal Propagation Trust, was established and agreed to explore existing information about these animals and to propose ways to breed them more successfully in captivity.

By 1970 the reality was becoming all too clear: the population scattered in nineteen American zoos had dropped to seventy. The animals were normally kept in large, mixed sex groups, and while nearly a third of the population had been born in zoos, captive-bred animals practically never bred in turn. Given the ten- to twenty-year life span of these creatures, all-out attrition was inevitable unless something was done. What was needed was information.

Practically nothing was known about these animals and their way of life. Brief research projects on marmosets and tamarins in the wild and some experiments in captivity showed that the diet most zoos supplied for them—chiefly fruit—was incorrect. They needed protein, lots of it, in the form of insects and other morsels enjoyed by the omnivorous. Shifting the tamarins' diet in favor of protein restored the natural reddishness of their fur; and still more important, increasing

In Brazil and throughout the tropics, access roads through forests permit and even encourage forest destruction. Many people enter the forest to log valuable hardwoods. Others burn patches of forest to create cropland and cattle pastures to eke out a marginal living.

the amount of vitamin D_3 they received through diet and exposure to sunlight brought the incidence of rickets under control. Mortality from fights was largely eliminated by housing adults as couples. But the rate of attrition of the captive population showed no sign of slowing, partly because these discoveries did not spread to all zoos immediately. In Brazil the picture was hardly rosier.

More of the Atlantic forest was falling daily to highway building, canals, ranches, and charcoal production. A new bridge allowed a quick commute between the high-rise apartments of urban Rio de Janeiro and trendy beach resorts; golden lion tamarin habitat was disappearing at an unabated rate. A two-part plan had been developed by Coimbra and several colleagues, but progress was slow. First, they had identified the single viable locale for a golden lion tamarin preserve, a twelve thousand–acre tract in the county of Silva Jardim called Poço das Antas, the "pool of the tapirs." At best, the area was a parlous haven, subject to burning and commercial hunting, host to a railroad that pierced its center, and far too expensive to be purchased by private funds. Only government intervention could secure the land for the tamarins. Second, Coimbra had conceived of a primate center to be erected in Tijuca National Park in the city of Rio de Janeiro where tamarins had preceded Cariocas long ago. Here tamarins from doomed tracts of forests could be kept and bred, with the hope of one day releasing them into the reserve or at least the surrounding park. Funds for the primate center were difficult to raise even with the World Wildlife Fund, the action arm of the IUCN, beating the drum. In 1970 a gloomy Coimbra had given the golden lion tamarins a mere three years in the wild.

Fifteen years later, in August 1985, I visited a tract of lowland tropical rain forest in Brazil as the guest of a group composed mostly of Brazilian students, volunteers, and Smithsonian scientists. We walked along a well-worn path that opened upon a clearing. In its center stood a tangle of naked tree trunks, broken branches, and shrubbery. A large cage, a golden tamarin halfway house, had once enclosed the tangle, but had since been removed.

High up on one tree trunk was a wooden nest box about three feet high and a foot deep. Bees were swarming in and out of it—Africanized bees, as they are called by scientists, or killer bees, as they have been dubbed in the American press. That very week California apiarists were warning each other that the arrival of millions of these aggressive, native African honeybees in a year or two from Mexico spelled doom, if not for the bee industry in general then at least for any hapless beekeeper who presumed to disturb the fierce new kids on the block. Here in the forest two Brazilian woodsmen in shorts and T-shirts, armed only with smokers, were preparing to climb the tree and eject the bees from the nest box of what was the second shipment of captive-bred golden lion tamarins to be released in the wild.

A young American zoologist, James Dietz, explained that they had found several instances of Africanized bee invasions of tamarin dens. Dietz and his wife, Lou Ann, were in the employ of the Smithsonian's National Zoological Park and together were the local directors of the

Key to the success of the captive breeding program was the discovery that tamarins live in family groups consisting of a monogamously mated adult pair and their young. All members of a family frequently huddle together, especially during mid-day resting periods.

Golden Lion Tamarin Conservation Project. While the woodsmen methodically smoked the bees and brushed them off their necks and faces, Dietz paused and said, "Hear that?"

From off in the distance came a high-pitched call, which I took to be that of a bird. "Here they come," said Dietz. We walked down the path deeper into the forest, and presently, overhead, there was a flash of red-gold, then another, and another. It was a group of golden lion tamarins, scampering through the branches, darting and leaping with the ease of natural gymnasts. They would pause to stare down, their naked greyish purple faces in a perpetual frown, curious but standoffish, even a bit imperious.

Nearby, a young Brazilian with binoculars began a soft staccato patter of information while a young colleague recorded it in symbols on a pad. They referred to the tamarins overhead by name, noting certain arcane aspects of their behavior. The names—Butterscotch and Lancelot—were familiar. Only a few months earlier I had watched these same tamarins darting back and forth in an enclosure behind the Small Mammal House at the National Zoo in Washington, D.C. They had been at the end of what is one of the more unusual education programs ever afforded a nonhuman primate. Now these same scholars were maneuvering happily in the subcanopy of the rain forest some five thousand miles south of Rock Creek Park. They were in the wild. Free. It was an exuberant moment for a new observer, and one felt that a philharmonic crescendo would have been altogether appropriate.

A few minutes later, the woodsmen descended the tree trunk with the den box, broke it open, and destroyed the remains of the bees' nest, while the last bees zipped irritatedly about their heads. The woodsman in charge had received a sting or two on his bare neck in the course of his depredations, but remained unruffled. He handed out bits of honeycomb. The honey was delicious, with a tang of orange to it, which was not surprising since this particular tract of forest, recently established as a preserve for the tamarin project and several miles from the Poço das Antas reserve, included a sizable orange grove.

While the bees grumbled off into the forest, Dietz explained that he and his wife were engaged in packing their belongings to return to the United States. In a few short years, the couple had gone from being referred to locally as *os Americanos* to the more affectionate *o pessoal do mico-leao*—the lion tamarin people. More important, they had trained a cadre of Brazilian zoologists and students in the principles and subtleties of tamarin-forest relations and were now leaving in properly local hands a widespread legacy of hope, possibility, understanding, and expertise in an arena often characterized by gloom. Fifteen years earlier, when Coimbra gave the tamarins only three years of existence in the wild, some corners had already been turned, however imperceptibly.

In 1972 the U.S. National Appeal of the World Wildlife Fund sent a small but important contribution of seed money for the primary center in Rio de Janeiro. By then a proclamation had been drawn up for the Brazilian president's signature, appropriating 12,400 acres at Poço das Antas to create the reserve—with plans for recompense to the owners. Additionally, a large working conference on the golden lion tamarins, including Coimbra and some Brazilian colleagues and specialists from American universities, zoos, and primate centers, had been slated to be held at the National Zoo in Washington. A number of important zoological and organizational principles emerged from this meeting.

It was agreed that while little was known about the behavior of golden lion tamarins, it was likely that insights about the behavior of any tamarin species were probably transferable. Also, it appeared to make little sense, from the standpoint of managing the entire zoo population of golden lion tamarins, to have them sprinkled here and there in many zoos, often with one adult pair to a zoo. For if a pair had young, the zoo would immediately have to arrange for other tamarins to be shipped in to provide the young with suitable mates. Further, the question of mate suitability involved such matters as inbreeding and the management not just of individual tamarins but of the flow of genes among them. Tamarin evolution had, in a sense, become the responsibility of humankind.

Workers at the Monkey Jungle in Florida, which maintained a sizable collection of these creatures, had found that a tamarin of mating age and inclination might ignore members of its own group and instead appear to court another individual from a nearby but separate cage. Brokering tamarin marriages was not a cut-and-dried business. Evidently, a step toward a solution was to concentrate the U.S. collection of these animals in a few larger colonies in zoos equipped for research and breeding. The idea of specialization, though not brand-new, ran counter to the traditional goal of most zoos to have as broad a range of animals as possible for exhibition.

As a result of the meeting at the National Zoo, zoos agreed to abide by a well-orchestrated, cooperative plan to increase the golden lion tamarin population. In this brave new endeavor, with the keen sup-

In a tamarin family, the mother carries her infants for their first few weeks of life. After that, carrying is largely left to the father. The infant this female, known as Sentinel, carries on her back was among the first born in the wild to a reintroduced animal.

port of then director Theodore Reed, the National Zoo took the lead. As a sign of its commitment, the zoo had just unveiled a new off-exhibit building. Originally planned for birds, the building would now house golden lion tamarins and be devoted exclusively to the study and breeding of these still mysterious creatures. (The marmoset building, as it was called by zoo staff, turned out, for reasons that later became clear, to be a well-meaning error.)

In this same year, 1972, the National Zoo had succeeded in a highly competitive effort to serve as the home for Ling-Ling and Hsing-Hsing, the giant pandas that came to symbolize the opening up of relations between the United States and the Peoples' Republic of China. These two media stars altogether overshadowed—in the public mind, at any rate—news of the tamarin project, but both soon became linked directly in the person of Devra Kleiman, a reproductive biologist hired to the zoo's research staff the same year as the tamarin conference and the giant pandas' arrival. Women zoologists were rare in those days, and Kleiman became the first on the zoo staff. She had worked previously with wolves and bats, becoming known serially as the Wolf Lady and the Bat Lady, and was soon to become known as the Panda Lady, with many of her days filled with frustration as the giant pandas, year in and year out, failed to reproduce. She might well have become known as the Tamarin Lady also, since in 1973 she took responsibility for the international effort to understand and breed these creatures and coordinated the field research and reintroduction that was to come.

Crucial to any such enterprise is the establishment of what might be thought of as the Scriptures, which dictate all action. In this case, the "golden tablet" that Kleiman took possession of is an unprepossessing volume called the International Golden Lion Tamarin Studbook. It had been drawn up by Marvin Jones of the San Diego Zoo during the late 1960s and provided, as far as information was available, the breeding history and genealogy of each captive tamarin beginning in 1960. Only through annual updating of the studbook can the complex task of maintaining the genetic health of the captive specimens be arranged.

In the beginning, of course, the studbook had many gaps. Nothing much was known of the genealogy of the wild-caught tamarins then in captivity, and they represented a large component of the captive population. Given the self-imposed ban on importing the animals, as well as the Brazilian export ban, the proportion of the population that was captive bred, and thus had a known genealogy, gradually increased. In 1975, however, the zoo population in the United States still seemed to be in a state of decline.

But even as this attrition continued, progress was being made in other areas of tamarin conservation. Careful observation of captive tamarin behavior, rigorous monitoring of their medical and nutritional needs, and other basic zoological research were turning up important clues to the difficult matter of getting the tamarins to breed more readily and keeping the resulting offspring viable.

Physical or emotional stress is obviously a roadblock to successful reproduction. What, then, causes stress among mating tamarins? They are believed to be monogamous, and left to their own devices, they

Golden lion tamarins are often found below the canopy of large, second-growth trees such as these in the Poço das Antas Reserve.

tend to live in nuclear family groups: a mating pair and its offspring. One of the causes of stress for a tamarin couple is the knowledge that there is another such couple nearby. It became clear that to reduce social tension, it was better to keep such groups isolated from each other. And since the tamarins were fragile in the face of certain diseases, especially those transmitted by humans, it was best to keep groups at different sites around the zoo to prevent the transmission of disease from one group to another. (Thus the marmoset building was eventually given over to multiple uses.)

Shortly after a tamarin gives birth, often to twins, occasionally to triplets, the young can be seen peering out from behind the mother's mane—an altogether endearing sight. Perhaps even more endearing is the restlessness the mother shows within a few days, when she begins to rub the infants off her back. Before long, if all goes well, the father will be seen doing his share of parental care, carrying the infants with him for part of the day and later presenting them with solid foods as weaning proceeds. In due course, the young from a previous litter also take up some of the chores of infant care. One aspect of this is a great deal of food sharing on the part of the adults and older siblings with the young—a behavior that is rare among mammals.

It turns out that permitting older juveniles to participate in infant rearing is of paramount importance if those juveniles are later to care adequately for their own young. To ensure that juvenile tamarins obtained this vital learning experience, the zoo would—when necessary—introduce hand-reared infants into the midst of an unrelated family. Such measures soon began to produce results.

But as with even the happiest of families there can be trouble. Among golden lion tamarins Kleiman learned the trouble often starts when female young reach puberty, sometimes even earlier. In many animals, including tamarins, the sheer presence of the parents can retard—for psychological and physiological reasons—the maturation of the young; but puberty inevitably does occur, at which point antagonism builds between a mother tamarin and her daughters, as well as among maturing sisters. Eventually, severe aggression occurs, often leading to injury and death if the two are forced to be in contact with each other. It could be conjectured, then, that in the wild the aggression between mother and daughter would lead to the ejection of pubertal females from the tamarin groups. The young females would then wander off to be absorbed into another neighboring group, thus passing around genes among families and reducing inbreeding. Answers to such questions awaited studies of wild populations, but in the meantime zoo keepers learned to keep a weather eye out and, at the first suggestion of intrasexual conflict, remove the youthful challenger and give her new quarters elsewhere.

Meanwhile, nutrition was improving. Reducing the quantity of fruit in the diet and substituting animal protein was beginning to have noticeable effects, and the tamarins were benefiting from ample doses of vitamin D_3. Once Kleiman became studbook keeper, she communicated regularly with all zoos holding golden lion tamarins so they had access to the latest research results and could apply the findings to their own programs. As a result of these significant and widespread

Stopping deforestation alone is not enough. Reforestation, or planting new trees and seedlings on cutover land, may be necessary to ensure sufficient habitat for future generations of tamarins.

nutritional changes, the average weight of an adult tamarin climbed from about 600 grams in the mid-1960s toward 750 grams a decade later.

Litter size also began to increase, with the average moving from 1.8 young per litter to more than two. (Currently, about one-fifth of all captive-born litters are triplets, and in 1981 a tamarin pair in the Los Angeles Zoo gave birth to the first recorded set of quadruplets.)

The population of golden lion tamarins began to climb. Between 1975 and 1980 the population doubled. By the end of that period, only four percent of the entire captive population had been born in the wild, and there were a number of fourth-generation captive-born specimens. Indeed, it became apparent by 1980 that the tamarin population would soon reach the maximum number for which there was likely to be proper space available in world zoos—about four hundred.

It had been noticed fairly early that relatively few progenitors (most of them from the National Zoo) had been responsible for a large proportion of the captive population, and careful manipulation of the stock, including a lot of trading and borrowing of animals between zoos, had broadened the genetic base of the population. Animals with common genetic backgrounds were removed from the breeding population and, conversely, those with rare genes were actively encouraged to breed. In 1980 more genetic depth was added to the North American group when Coimbra sent up five new tamarins from the primate center in Brazil.

Even so, the gene pool was dangerously limited, and among the captive population, zoo scientists and veterinarians had already found a possible genetic time bomb. Six percent of the population—including animals from five different institutions—suffered from the same anatomical defect, a kind of hernia. In this condition, a defect of the diaphragm, the liver and intestines push into the chest cavity, resulting in what is called, in the cool lingo of science, "reduced viability." It turned out that the hernia might not be a result of inbreeding, as it was found in groups that were not closely related genetically, and, equally troubling, Kleiman could not produce animals with hernias by selectively breeding for the trait. Eliminating it could prove impossible and reducing its incidence extremely difficult.

Nevertheless, in the early 1980s, Jonathan Ballou, the National Zoo's population manager and the new studbook keeper, and other scientists from the several institutions with golden lion tamarin holdings were looking at what was about to be an exponential growth. The animal future, at least in captivity, could be said to be secure, but the price of an extraordinary success was the sudden and urgent need to put on the reproductive brakes, lest the population swell to what one estimate put at 3,500 animals by 1990—far too many for zoos to maintain and, in fact, severe overpopulation. This called for consideration of various measures, including breaking up mating pairs and active sterilization procedures, such as vasectomy and hormone implants. Euthanasia of genetically overrepresented individuals was even considered. Meanwhile, with the certainty of a surplus of active tarmarins looming before them, the International Management Committee for the Golden Lion Tamarin began to cast its eyes more often toward

Poco das Antas, the reserve in Brazil. The notion of returning captive-bred golden lion tamarins to the wild tugged ever more forcefully at the minds of their American benefactors.

Such attempts had been made before in South America with monkey species, including squirrel monkeys and other tamarin species, but introductions were a risky business. One difficulty was the failure of captive animals to cope with so radically different an environment; another was the extreme unpleasantness that often arose when captive populations ran into wild populations. Indeed, the entire practice was shrouded in uncertainty, because previous attempts had not included careful day-to-day monitoring of the animals once they were set free. Still, Poço das Antas beckoned, a somewhat disheveled siren, but a siren nonetheless.

It can be a hair-raising experience to drive along Highway 101 from Rio de Janeiro to the turnoff for the Poço das Antas Biological Reserve. Whoever owns the dealership for Mercedes trucks in this area must be among Brazil's wealthiest citizens, for literally hundreds of these behemoths barrel by the tentative driver, even passing two abreast at times, thundering by into blind curves. As one drives warily northeast in an alcohol-powered Volkswagon, cities become towns, then settlements, then remote single dwellings. Here and there the road is lined with clusters of ceramics factories with woodfired kilns, reminders that most of this strip was once forest land. Now it is given over to scrubby-looking farmland and pasture and to the occasional eroded hillside. By law, slopes are not supposed to be deforested nowadays, but most still are, and they become mini-moonscapes with the first rains. Fires alongside the highway burn untended, turning new woodland into impoverished pasture. The turn-off to the reserve is easily missed: it leads past more farm buildings and fires to a gate, beyond which is a house. One stops and waits, and eventually a guard exits the house and opens the gate to the reserve. If the guard is not home, the instructions are to simply wait there in the car until he arrives.

The reserve itself, located in the foothills of the Serra do Mar and formally established in 1974 by presidential decree, languished for a number of years as deforestation, further development, and poaching continued and as fire ravaged large portions of it. A director for the reserve, Dionisio Pessamilio, was finally appointed in 1977, and with the addition of a small staff of guards, the remaining forest in the reserve had a chance of being saved. By 1980, only forty percent of the reserve could be considered useful tamarin habitat, and censuses suggested that there were only one hundred golden lion tamarins in the reserve. So small a number, in itself, was disquieting, posing the likelihood of rampant inbreeding in the wild population. Wildlife managers were beginning to recognize that wild populations restricted to isolated preserves differed little in many respects from captive populations in zoos. Both needed direct genetic intervention and management.

In 1981 Devra Kleiman met with Brazilian counterparts and together they developed a multipronged approach to save golden lion tamarins

and remedy the problems of Poço das Antas, the only place in the world set aside for their survival in the wild. What was needed, simply, were trees, research, and education. Degradation of the land had to be replaced by restoration and reforestation. Scientists had to learn more about the natural behavior and ecology of the golden lion tamarin. And the people of the region had to be considered: a conservation education program had to be undertaken to create public awareness of the tamarin and its needs and, perhaps, to kindle local pride in what were obviously some fairly heroic last-ditch efforts. Within months the "pool of the tapir" became the site of a remarkable crash course in salvage zoology.

Uniquely suited to undertake such a task on the scene were James and Lou Ann Dietz. James was a young biologist experienced in working with endangered species in wildlife preserves in Brazil, Lou Ann, a gifted teacher. Both were fluent in Portuguese, the language of Brazil. Employed by the National Zoo, they moved in May 1983 into a ramshackle, bat-filled farmhouse on the reserve, which quickly became a site of feverish activity to rival the nests of the Africanized bees.

While the house was rebuilt amid seasonal rains that turned the yard to mire, an outbuilding was converted into a laboratory, willing students were recruited, and detailed observations of the resident tamarins began—a matter of standing and watching hour after hour, day after day, for weeks and months. At the same time, hundreds of acres were dosed with lime, in the hope that if the soil were improved and the ravages of fire controlled, if not eliminated, the reserve could restore itself in the natural course of things. Experimental plots were cordoned off and studied: no one knew much about how a former rain forest, once a place of amazing diversity of plant species, could reemerge from desolate grassland.

The tamarins were relentlessly tracked and, sometimes, trapped and put through exhaustive physicals, many leaving the laboratory with radio transmitters affixed to collars. A fuller picture of the life of tamarins revealed itself.

Certain fears were confirmed. Blood samples, sent to Washington, D.C., for biochemical analysis of blood proteins, suggested that the wild population of tamarins at Poco das Antas was indeed more inbred than the captive population in the United States—a compelling argument for the introduction of captive-bred animals back into the wild.

The status of the wild population in the reserve was now estimated at about 115 animals, with perhaps another 300 barely surviving in tiny forest patches on private lands. Only 45 had home ranges exclusively within the reserve; the other 70 ranged both within and beyond the reserve's borders. All told, there were about fifteen bands in isolated pockets of forest separated by open land. They had probably been inbreeding for years, Dietz noted, adding, "We may have to manage the gene lines of wild populations like we do those in captivity." It was evident that the reserve, as then configured, could not support a genetically viable population of tamarins. The minimum size for such a population, it was assumed, would range between 300 and 500 animals.

Stars of The Tamarin Trickster, *a play written and performed by Brazilians to dramatize the plight of golden lion tamarins and all the creatures of the disappearing forest. This play was one of many educational and promotional activities developed as part of the Golden Lion Tamarin Conservation Project.*

(Previous page) Deforestation's devastating impact on flashy primates is well documented, but whether and how many tropical forest invertebrates have already become extinct may never be known.

Wild tamarins, it became clear, usually live in familial groups with a sex ratio of one to one, with one pair of breeding adults per group. Monogamy seems to be the wild tamarin style. Each group has a home range of about one hundred acres, with the ranges of adjacent groups overlapping by about ten percent. The animals use holes in trees for denning: some groups have as many as twenty dens throughout their home range. They spend most of their waking time in the branches and vines below the forest canopy. There they are relatively safe from avian predators such as hawks, as well as from ground-dwelling enemies such as the occasional jaguarundi, ocelot, or puma, and the more dangerous and prevalent free-ranging domestic dogs. Ideal tamarin habitat consists of swampy forest with trees full of epiphytes, those remarkable tropical plants that live, roots and all, on trees. Many epiphytes, such as certain species of bromeliads, form useful receptacles for rainwater in which insects and small vertebrates like frogs—sources of high-quality protein—often live. Above two hundred meters altitude, epiphytes become sparser with their water evaporating quickly during the dry season, which suggests why golden lion tamarins are not found beyond this frontier.

One group of Brazilian students was assigned to collect, pickle, and census all the animal life to be found in bromeliads and other epiphytes that grew within a long swath through the reserve. Another group set about analyzing the status of the rare maned sloth and other species that were now benefiting from the protection given to Poço das Antas. The data obtained from such studies were deemed of primary importance. The actual training of Brazilian students in the techniques and principles of wildlife management was equally crucial since, for obvious reasons, the management of the reserve and the tamarins would have to become a Brazilian affair. Indeed, a major goal was to develop an ongoing program that could be administered indigenously.

Meanwhile, an entire nearby citizenry—some eighty-nine thousand people—had to be educated. Lou Ann Dietz, aided by Elizabeth Nagagata, a Brazilian of Japanese extraction, began a courteous, if insistent, blitz, exploring every opportunity to bring the tamarin message to local schools, landowners, and politicians, inviting local participation in planning the reserve's future and solving its problems, and employing every available medium from local television to sophisticated graphics, parades, opinion polls, school plays, and posters. The tamarin was used explicitly and deliberately as a symbol for preservation of natural habitat in general and has made its way, via the Brazilian press's fascination with it, into the national consciousness. The tamarin project logo, developed in Washington, D.C., by the National Zoo's graphics department, can now be found adorning the walls of local Brazilian service stations and other unlikely spots for miles around the reserve. The education program has been directly responsible for a dramatic increase in the number of tamarins donated to the reserve and the number of reports to the authorities of tamarins illegally held in captivity.

The reintroduction of captive-bred tamarins to the wild became a real possibility largely because of this consciousness raising. Land

with suitable tamarin habitat but, for one reason or another, no tamarins was desperately needed. At first some forest within the reserve
was found where captive-bred animals could be introduced without
immediately running afoul of wild groups. But this land was not
enough to support the three hundred to five hundred tamarins considered necessary for a genetically viable population. Later, local ranch
owners, as a result of the education program, donated patches of forest to the golden lion tamarin in exchange for a tax write-off and a
justifiable sense of civic pride. As land became available, preparations
in Washington took on more life.

Yet before any zoo-born tamarins could be transferred to the
wild, more education was imperative. National Zoo primatologist Benjamin Beck assumed the role of master teacher in
a tamarin "outward bound" program. The first class, in 1983, enrolled
fifteen pupils, a group of tamarins from the National Zoo and from
four others—King's Island in Ohio, Brookfield in Chicago, the Los Angeles Zoo, and the San Antonio Zoo. The pupils were, in effect, pam-
pered city kids who needed to learn survival skills for a wholly different world, a wilderness. They had never searched for food, but had
had it presented—literally on a platter—on a regular daily schedule. If
any had ever caught an insect, it was a cockroach or a farm-raised
cricket. Here, then, were fifteen monkeys who did not comprehend
the business of peeling a banana. Foraging became the first and chief
required course.

Beck and his assistants among the zoo keeper corps began hiding
food—mealworms, fruit, and so forth—around the tamarins' enclosures, secreting it in crevices, taping it to the bottom of branches,
packaging it in toilet paper rolls. When the animals eventually caught
on, Beck would leave some packages and hiding places empty so the
tamarins would learn to handle disappointment and continue probing.
Such behavior deserved a scientific term; Beck dubbed it "micromanipulation." The easy predictable life was over.

"We also had to teach them that unlike zoo structures, tree branches
come in varying widths, strengths, and textures," said Beck. The tamarins soon found themselves swaying uncomfortably on thin, flexible branches after a leap onto what they had always assumed was a
solid perch.

In December 1983 the scholars were sent to Coimbra's primate
center, where the training intensified, still under Beck's watchful
tutorial eye. A female bit a proffered poisonous toad, planning to eat
it, and needed immediate medical care when convulsions began. Subsequently, upon seeing the same toad in a glass jar, the female attacked it with the same verve, evidently still intent on eating it. Some
lessons, it seemed, were not easily learned.

Overflying birds and bird silhouettes made the tamarins duck auto-
matically, dropping down into the branches—behavior that could be
considered "hard-wired" in tamarin genes. But unpeeled bananas
were treated with about as much interest as rocks until the tamarins
became adept at peeling them. Besides learning the gustatorial values
of local fruits, it was important for them to learn about more animated

*Saving a species takes the combined
efforts of many people. Shown below
are some of the members of the Golden
Lion Tamarin Project team at the Poço
das Antas Reserve.*

Providing food so that zoo tamarins would have to search for it proved to be a time-consuming chore for their keepers (above). Used to having their meals in bowls full of bite-sized chunks of food, zoo tamarins had to be taught how to forage for prey and even how to open and eat a banana (right) in preparation for their return to the wild.

food, such as insects, frogs, and small lizards. These had to be provided by Beck and his associates, so hunting up such creatures became full-time work. Even so, human primates simply are not as efficient in this as wild tamarins, and four of the golden lion tamarins died at the primate center, three of them evidently unable to adapt to a protein-rich cereal offered at the center. The struggle for independence has ever been nothing if not arduous.

One wild-caught tamarin donated to the primate center was added to the group of pioneers and adjusted well, and two young were born there to a captive-bred pair, bringing the total to fourteen by May 1984, when eight were taken to Poço das Antas and placed in the wire-mesh halfway house to acclimatize themselves to the sounds and smells of their ultimate home. At the end of the month the trapdoor was opened, the first male emerged. The scientists barely contained their cheers. Within a few days, the halfway house was removed, depriving the tamarins of their nightly retreat and also a favored perch, which was adjudged to be too open to avian predation. In due course, the denning box brought from the zoo was taken over by bees, forcing the animals to seek out their own den sites in trees. Meanwhile, food proffered daily by the reserve staff was diminished, and within eighteen months the survivors were finding approximately eighty-five percent of their food by themselves. All the while, Dietz's band of zoology students were spending hours monitoring not only the tamarins' food intake, but also the directions they traveled into the surrounding forest and the distance from the site of the original halfway house they achieved. Within six weeks of the original release of eight, the remaining six were also turned loose.

By March 1985 five of the fourteen first released were still free-ranging in Poço das Antas. A hunter's dog had got one, a snake another. One, exiled by social conflicts, had spent a night out in the elements and died of exposure, and two had simply disappeared. One other had to be removed when conflict broke out between two released groups, and others died from an undetermined medical affliction. Was this success? Beck thought so, and he was further buoyed by the fact that on December 18, 1984, the first baby tamarin born in the wild of captive-bred parents had appeared. "This kid," Beck told a reporter at the time, "will grow up as a wild golden lion tamarin. It will never know captivity."

As it turned out, that infant soon died but was later replaced in another group by twins, one of whom has now had babies in the wild herself. Yet, mortality was considerable and continued. Only three of the original fourteen pioneers are still alive, but they have now produced and reared seven offspring. In the minds of the Golden Lion Tamarin Conservation Project scientists, successful reproduction constitutes successful reintroduction. Also, the methodology for reintroducing such animals into wild habitat is beginning to be understood. Dietz calls it a "technology," and to the extent that it becomes another tool in the kit of animal conservationists, the term is apt.

In the summer of 1985, two more groups of golden lion tamarins, one group having received a now slightly refined outward bound course in Washington and in Brazil, were released—not in the reserve proper but in a nearby tract called Pesagro that contained orange groves. In August the group that had received training—Lancelot and Butterscotch's crowd—appeared to be doing well, ranging as far as 250 meters from home base.

Across the tract of forest in a similar clearing was the other group. They were in the daily care of a young Brazilian zoology student named Inês Castro, and they confronted their new world without much enthusiasm. Indeed, to an untrained eye, they seemed just a bit dismayed. Like a human outward bound class, they had been thrust into the wilds without previous training. They would learn on the job in a rather different kind of experiment. Training the tamarins in a captive situation was time-consuming, labor-intensive, and therefore expensive. Beck and his assistants had wondered if on-the-job training might not be as effective and less expensive.

The group of four, a matriarch named Maria and three youthful tamarins, of which a male named Juan, the youngest, found himself at the very bottom of the pecking order, were homebodies compared to the other recently released group. So far they had ranged a mere forty meters from the clearing—in fact, only Maria had ventured this far, and only on one occasion. "We were so happy," recalled Castro. Maria's feat was, in fact, out of character: among the other groups of released tamarins, it had been the adults that were conservative while the more youthful members would venture farther and try new foods, showing the way to their reluctant elders. Here, in the untrained group, it was Maria who was the experimental one.

Castro was a patient wilderness guide. She would spend about eight hours a day in the clearing, watching the animals and recording their every move. The area was broken down into sections with direction and distance markers. The zoologist noted how far they would roam and in which direction, what they caught, what they ate, and which of their companions they were nearest to whenever they did something noteworthy.

Early on, Castro had built a platform out of bamboo and placed it about five feet off the ground in the clearing. It was full of empty places where food could be secreted; Beck termed it a "portable micromanipulation platform," or PMP. After gaining experience on this special platform, as well as at natural places here and there that Castro would selectively seed with various foodstuffs or fraudulently bait with leaves, the neophytes had begun to forage on their own. Daily, Castro would secrete food in bamboo sticks, natural crevices, and bromeliads farther and farther away from the clearing in the direction of a swampy area where, it was hoped, these tamarins would finally center their home range.

Between stints of methodical observation, Castro explained that this group ate less natural food than the other Pesagro group but also moved less—they had at the time reached only seven meters above ground. Thus they lost less weight than their highly active neighbors. They seemed a long way from a condition of wildness, approaching even a strange human to within a couple of feet and staring imperiously, or happily unzipping and micromanipulating the contents of a

camera bag sitting on the ground. And when Castro left briefly, returning with a sack of oranges, "science diet," and bananas, the tamarins knew just what was up. Not only was it feeding time, it was nearing the end of their day.

Castro placed the precisely weighed food in various spots around the clearing, eagerly pursued by the tamarins. Juan, the youngest, leapt up to a fork in a branch where half an orange had been placed. He was immediately screamed at by his brother Pepe, who appropriated the orange, leaving Juan to go off unsteadily, emitting a rasping sound that Castro explained is an infantile vocalization tamarins hold onto later in life to signal that they are being threatened or "need toleration."

It was about two o'clock in the afternoon. Castro had been with the group since sunup, patiently watching, recording, hoping. Several tamarins were heading for the next box attached to a tree. Off in the forest there was a distant roar, a continuous sound. "That must be those killer bees," said Castro, "looking for another place to nest."

She picked up her empty sack. "These tamarins," she said, "go to bed around two-thirty every afternoon. The other groups stay up till dusk." She smiled. Across the clearing a tamarin named Jackie had found another orange.

I wandered down the path away from the clearing, trailing Inês Castro and worrying idly about Juan, the lowest-rung dweller, a real tamarin, an actual, individual monkey thrust into what must seem an altogether discouraging real world. At one point during the day Juan had stopped a few feet away on a branch and had screamed at me with apparent outrage. I had flinched, hoping with utter anthropomorphism that it had given him at least one opportunity that day to feel like a big shot.

Juan and the others were palpable living creatures, but they were symbols too. In a sense, the entire program of introducing tamarins into the wild is symbolic. The managers of this project are quick to emphasize that reintroduction is, at best, a small part of the overall attempt to save the golden lion tamarin—a dramatic part to be sure, and an exercise that might well extend the gene pool of the wild groups, as well as an exercise from which a prodigious amount of practical zoology is being learned—a new technology. But the introduction program was designed also as a means to draw attention to the entire tamarin effort, to dramatize the urgent need to save habitat.

A month earlier, in July 1985, the Brazilian government had declared that a 450-mile strip of Atlantic forest to the south, in the state of São Paulo, was henceforth a protected national landmark, and negotiations were underway to extend the classification to the entire 1,200-mile Serra do Mar mountain range, in the foothills of which lies Poço das Antas. "This is the first time in Latin America that an entire region has been protected," said Thomas Lovejoy of the World Wildlife Fund–U.S. at the time. It seemed fair, walking through the forest that day, to believe that Juan and his reluctant fellows, symbols all—and the abstract likeness of the golden lion tamarin created by the National Zoo's graphics department, and the thousands upon thousands of hours devoted to these few vivid, lively creatures—had

(Left) A bowl of human-prepared food supplemented the diets of recently released tamarins until they perfected their ability to forage for themselves in the wild.

(Below) Micueca, a wild-born male who was among the first tamarins to be reintroduced, carries twin infants born about ten months after his return to the wild.

(Top) Led by James Dietz and Benjamin Beck, the tamarin team heads determinedly into the forest to begin the first-ever reintroduction of zoo-born tamarins into the wild.

(Middle) Few details of the lives of reintroduced or soon to be reintroduced golden lion tamarins went unrecorded. Here Benjamin Beck takes notes on the behavior of an outward bound group of tamarins.

(Bottom) Nest boxes placed in trees at the release site formed home bases for tamarin groups, as well as provided a sleep shelter and some protection from predators.

(Right) Carrying twins born in the wild, this reintroduced female still enjoyed melons and other food items furnished to the tamarins (above). Eventually, however, the tamarins relied on natural foods, such as insects and small frogs that live in the water that collects on the tops of bromeliads (below).

Resting in a tree overhung with epi-phytes, this golden lion tamarin seems to be contemplating life in a Brazilian forest. We can only imagine the feelings of the tamarins who found themselves suddenly free to live—and die—in the wild, in their ancestral home. But for the people who carried out the tamarin project, and for all those who care about wildlife, these beautiful animals' return to the wild evokes a thrill of pride and a surge of hope for the future of all such biological treasures.

played some significant role in what Lovejoy called "a major positive step" in the often disheartening scenery of wildlife conservation.

Given the nature of things, Juan's personal long-term future was by no means assured, nor was that of his fellow outward-bounders, nor even that of their wild-born kin. Poço das Antas could still one day prove too small or too fragile to maintain a viable tamarin gene pool. And there will always be those greedy, amoral folk who seek profits in such matters: golden lion tamarins remain popular pets in various parts of Asia and are still found in the illicit animal trade, a trade so nefarious that most other smugglers even consider it vile.

Nonetheless, for now, at least, these tamarins and their fragment of rain forest are a reddish gold ray of light, an encouragement to say that the glass is half full instead of half empty. There can be nothing wrong with being such a symbol, especially when progress seems so real. Sixty-seven tamarins have now been released in Poço das Antas and surrounding areas, more than a dozen young have been born in the wild to these animals, and survivorship is running about fifty percent.

There was a time—just years ago—when most zoos were places where for understandable and admirable reasons exotic animals were selectively extracted from the wild and assembled almost exclusively for exhibit purposes. In recent years, another dimension has been added to the world of the zoo—one might say there has been a revolution. Many zoos have become places of rigorous scientific research, both pure and applied, coupled with an active effort not just to preserve in captivity those creatures that are endangered in the wild, but to cooperate with each other and with other nations to understand, save, and replenish unique natural habitats.

No longer can anyone complain that zoos are extractive industries. They are rapidly fulfilling their role as institutions of a particularly needed kind of education and they guide the rest of us along the path of active stewardship of life.

For what can be thought of, then, as the new zoo, the golden lion tamarin, with its brilliant pelage and its fierce expression, makes a fine symbol indeed—a fitting semaphore of human energy and commitment.

ACTIVE ANIMALS

Elephants are thick-skinned and highly sensitive. They like to be praised, even applauded. They are the most charismatic inhabitants of the Elephant House, which they share with giraffes, hippos, and rhinos (also pretty charismatic). Nancy is a thirty-five-year-old African elephant weighing 10,000 pounds, Ambika is a forty-year-old Asian elephant weighing 8,400 pounds, and Shanti is a thirteen-year-old Asian elephant also weighing 8,400 pounds. Together these elephants inhabit three interior enclosures and a large, relatively barren yard. It's barren because they keep it that way. Elephants routinely knock down trees and eat them. Zoo horticulturists once planted a few in the moat around the Elephant House, but these failed to survive the attentions of the elephants' prehensile trunks, which are awesomely powerful but capable of amazing delicacy. With some 100,000 muscles and tendons in its trunk, an elephant can with ease pick up an object the size of a pencil, aided by two "fingers" on the end of the trunk in the African elephant and one in the Asian. Asian elephants differ from African elephants in a number of other characteristics. Their tusks do not show, their ears are smaller, and the highest point on their body is the middle of their back, as opposed to the shoulder on the African elephants.

In 1988 Nancy, the African elephant that had been alone for thirteen years, was put together with the two Asian elephants, and the three quickly formed a bond. In the wild, female elephants are rarely if ever alone and need social contact for their emotional health. And in a zoo environment, they need entertainment as well. There is a daily "treasure hunt" when the keepers hide enjoyable morsels around the cage to challenge the animals. The elephants are bread "junkies" and are indulged in this during the hunt—a supplement to the daily diet of timothy hay, fruit, vegetables, and tree branches.

Each day the elephants also participate in three different educational programs, narrated by volunteers from FONZ (Friends of the National Zoo), a private, nonprofit organization that is in many ways part of the zoo's lifeblood. In the morning one of the elephants is led across the moat to meet the public up close. Later on, the keepers demonstrate how they work on the animals' feet to keep them fit and how the elephants flatten aluminum cans for one of the zoo's recycling programs. And then the keepers show their control over the elephants, leading them through a "workout" that includes moving heavy logs around the enclosure.

In the wild an elephant may walk twenty-five miles a day foraging for some 350 pounds of food. In a zoo such a trek is impossible and as a result dead skin builds up on the elephants' feet and their toenails don't get worn down. So they must permit their "boss," or keeper, to manipulate their feet: once a week the dead skin is shaved off and the toenails filed. A strong social bond between elephant and keepers, formed out of constant contact, is essential if the keepers are to maintain control over the animals, and it is on that control that keepers' safety and the animals' health depends. The daily routines are entertaining for the elephants and for visitors, but they are also part of the continuing exercise of authority. During the fun, an ankus, or hook, is always in sight. "You use it so that you won't have to really use it," the keepers say. "They know when they've done something wrong, and they expect appropriate discipline. They also know when they should be praised and they expect that too. It's how you earn their love and respect."

The zoo today, just like Nancy and the other three or four thousand animals who live there, is a product of its own evolution. And just as a paleontologist can look at an elephant and see what might be remnants of the species from which the elephant arose, one can see remnants of the National Zoo's earlier ages. Indeed, on the western edge of the zoo, one can still discern the remains of a round bear pit that, in the 1890s, was the accepted way of exhibiting bears and other large zoo animals. A bear pit certainly kept the bears away from people, but it had three distinct disadvantages: it was bad for the animals, bad for the visitor (who could only see the animals from above), and practically impossible for the animal keeper. How do you clean up a pit full of bears?

Putting animals inside moats, an idea evidently inspired by the moats around European towns, gave the animals more room but shared all of the pit's difficulties. Putting animals at ground level, surrounded by heavy wooden fences, was well and good except that it obscured the visitor's view. By the turn of the century, iron bars and wire mesh had become the state of the art in zoo exhibiting. The cages at the Monkey House, built in 1907, reflect this era. Shortly thereafter, Carl Hagenbeck, a German animal trainer, developed the

Zoo elephants need the company of other elephants—and of the keepers who become "honorary" members of the herd—daily baths to keep their skin soft and supple, and the opportunity to keep busy through work such as moving logs or even just entertaining visitors.

idea of using a naturalistic setting, surrounded by an impassable moat. Virtually every zoo ever since has been working out modifications and variations of Hagenbeck's theme. Each zoo exhibit reflects a necessary compromise between three main considerations: the animal's needs, the visitor's need to see the animal, and the requirements of keepers and others who must daily intervene (with safety for both parties) in the animal's life. There are other restrictions too that have to be made in producing an animal exhibit that will serve these needs. Every zoo has some space limitations—especially urban zoos—and also financial limitations. Yet other factors are topography and climate. The National Zoo lies in the sharply rising hills and plunging gorges of Rock Creek Park. Even if the zoo were suddenly, in some magical way, to double its area, there is no way that one could produce an American Bison exhibit that looked much like the Great Plains. Climate plays an important role too in the zoo's architecture. Washington's relatively cold winters mean that tropical animals must be able to get indoors—some must be indoors at all times. Giant pandas, cold-weather animals from the mountains of Tsechuan, are debilitated by the region's hot and humid summers and seek relief indoors in an air conditioned shelter (as most Washingtonians do).

Among the pleasures of visiting a zoo, one is to see how, from exhibit to exhibit, the zoo's designers and scientists and keepers have provided for the needs of the animal, the visitor, and the keeper.

Most of the mammals encountered in the zoo need times of privacy. It has been said of the National Zoo that it is one of the most humane of zoos in that it does provide such privacy. Benjamin Beck, a primatologist and assistant director for exhibits at the zoo, likes to explain that "the animals themselves decide whether to be on exhibit." Most of the mammal enclosures have places where the animal can, at will, find privacy from the viewing public—a hiding place, or a separate den.

Such is the case a short walk up the hill from the Elephant House to what is certainly the most popular spot in the zoo: the Panda House, the home of Ling-Ling and Hsing-Hsing. In 1972, when they arrived, these pandas were more than just two animals. They were symbols. The gift of the Peoples' Republic of China to the people of the United States, they symbolized a new and more comfortable era in international relations. (In return, the United States delivered two musk oxen to the Chinese, animals the Peking Zoo was particularly anxious to have.) The pandas immediately became the darlings of the press and TV—and commerce. Pandas appeared on the shelves of virtually every kind of retail establishment. One perfume company got a little PR by pronouncing the two animals "Sweethearts of the Year." As Larry Collins, their first curator, said, it was "pandamonium."

With amazing dispatch, a building that had housed hoofed stock was remodeled, not only to accommodate the pandas but also the enormous crowds that, predictably, came. Each animal had its separate, adjacent indoor and outdoor enclosure. Each had its own private den to which it could go at will. Many visitors who came specifically to see the pandas were disappointed to find them missing: they were young and toddled off to their dens to sleep quite a bit of the time.

Spacious, open enclosures that give zoo animals like Ling-Ling (left) room both to romp and to relax have replaced the small, iron-barred cage of the old-style zoo (above).

(Following page) Witnessing a baby's birth thrills zoo staff and visitors alike. Dozens of people attended this birth of a dama gazelle—giving the casual visitor a rare treat and providing parents and children with a unique opportunity to chat about one of life's most significant events.

But for millions of visitors, Ling-Ling and Hsing-Hsing (which mean Little Girl and Bright Star) fulfilled their promise. There is something inherently cute about a giant panda, with its slightly silly black ears, apparent smile, and black eye patches. These, which make the animal appear to have great big eyes, engender the same affectionate response humans experience on seeing the relatively large eyes of babies. There is something inherently funny about pandas too. One can only smile at a black-and-white bear sitting, leaning back against a wall with hind legs splayed out, holding an apple or a piece of bamboo in one front paw (which because of a peculiar configuration of the wrist seems almost to have an opposable thumb) and contentedly scratching its stomach with the other paw. These antics, plopping into a tub of water, batting a durable plastic ball around the outdoor enclosure, seemed even to their keepers to be deliberate clowning, similar to antics that make parents laugh at their children at play. For the pandas' benefit, and for the benefit of zoo visitors, the National Zoo undertook several years later to build them elaborate jungle gyms in their outdoor enclosures. Responding to a plea from FONZ, seven hundred members of the Washington community responded: the playground equipment was designed and built entirely by volunteers. To this day it provides needed exercise for the animals and entertainment for the visitors.

The pandas soon became symbols of the difficulty of dealing with another culture—in this case, the culture of little-known animals. Truly very little was known about the panda, either in the wild or in captivity. Few if any field studies had been carried out in the panda's native habitat, the cold, remote bamboo forests of the mountains in southwestern China. Those few animals that had existed in Western zoos had, with few exceptions, not been systematically studied. Though pandas had bred in captivity in China, Chinese zoo people had scanty scientific information to share with the Americans about this important matter. So the zoo was essentially flying blind. The story of the pair's inability to have young has been a long and, of course, frustrating one, but as a result of the highly systematic efforts by zoo researchers, keepers, and volunteer observers from FONZ, Ling-Ling and Hsing-Hsing have yielded, if not young pandas, certainly more basic biological information about the species than had accumulated in all of history. The story of this research effort is reserved for a later chapter. For now, let it suffice that the Panda House is one of many places where one sees the compromises involved in sharing an exotic animal's life with an interested public. The charge for exhibiting animals at the zoo, as it has been formulated by National Zoo Director Michael Robinson, is "active animals doing interesting things." But some animals also require one degree or another of privacy, so everyone—from animals to visitors—is daily involved in these gentle tradeoffs.

In the area surrounding the Panda and the Elephant houses are denizens of perhaps less charisma but worth knowing nonetheless. These are the hoofed stock, some hardy, some delicate, all the product of millions of years of evolution, always one

(Previous page) American bison and sandhill cranes share a snowy enclosure at the zoo just as they share similar habitats on the Great Plains of the American West.

(Below) Despite its tropical origins, a sloth bear appears comfortable in the snow of a Washington winter.

(Right) Washingtonians find a peaceful stroll through the snow-shrouded park one way to escape the clamor of the nation's capital.

dangerous link below the big carnivores in the food chain. The more delicate, the more they remain—even here in these safe confines— alert and ready to flee. The sturdy American bison, however, seems not to have a care in the world, often found lying placidly chewing his cud. His kind is only recently returned to the zoo, adding a nice bit of historical continuity since it was a small herd of bison, rescued from oblivion in the 1880s by a farsighted Smithsonian biologist named Hornaday, and housed in pens on the Mall, that gave rise to the National Zoo.

Nearby is a small herd of Dorcas gazelles, often given to nervous jostling, especially when it is time, on three occasions each year, for them to be herded into the arms of keepers and veterinarians for the regular series of shots that protect them from disease. They are adept not only at evasive action—the roundups are often nearly slapstick affairs—but at masking any symptoms of disease. They can look fine one day and be dead the next. It takes specially careful observation by their keepers to monitor their health. Just how healthy they are is attested to by the fact that these gazelles are among the most productive breeders of all the hoofed stock: stressed animals rarely breed.

Generally speaking, this is a quiet part of the zoo, a contemplative place and one of the few in the busy city that surrounds it. Up the hill from the Panda House one can stand on ground among the highest points in this city of seven hills and quietly observe some of the world's finest athletes in repose. The bongo, for example. Its name seems as if it had come from old Tarzan strips, but there is nothing commonplace about it. Splendid muscles ripple under a dark coppery brown coat lined vertically with white strips. The head is brown, with a white mask over the eyes and a black nose, a mask that reminds you of exotic African ceremonies. The horns are bent and crossed like an upside down plié. This large antelope watches you with superior calm, standing in perfect conformation, front legs together, rear legs stretched slightly back, ready to run but obviously seeing no threat. Up on the hill it is not hard to get into the mood: far enough away to be irrelevant is the swish of traffic past the elegant apartment buildings of Connecticut Avenue. One can forget the cares of the day and also the fact that the bongo is in trouble as a species in its native land of Kenya, the victim of drought and the still inexplicable need of man to make war on his neighbors.

The bongos, along with others of the hoofed stock, such as giraffes and Dorcas gazelles, are breeding successfully at the zoo. Others— like the Bactrian camel and zebra—are on display here for purely educational reasons: members of their species are actively breeding in the zoo's Conservation and Research Center, a breeding farm not open to the public and located two hours drive west in the Blue Ridge Mountains.

These hoofed animals are not superstars in the culture of the zoogoer, not what zoo people themselves call "charismatic megafauna," but they evolved in grasslands—developing the four-chambered stomach that permits ungulates to eat grass and the long legs for running over hard, flat country. In their presence one can reflect that it is also in the vicinity of grasslands that we became human: we have been

(Left) Sumatran tigers are the last of three subspecies of island tigers—Bali and Java tigers became extinct in the past twenty years. The zoo focuses on breeding these endangered animals.

(Above) The preferred activity of lions—in the wild as in the zoo—is lolling around in the grass. Well-fed adult lions seldom show the slightest interest in moving between meals.

looking at these animals throughout our history as a species.

No zoo would be complete in the public mind without the next step up in the food chain—the large carnivores, in particular, the big cats. Few zoo exhibits are as elementally thrilling as the sight of lions and tigers striding about, the gods of the feline world as even the most devoted domestic cat owner would have to admit. The terraced hill, where a visitor can belly up to a low wall and look across a moat at one of these enormous animals close up—perhaps even catch a tiger having a swim—is one of the most popular spots in the National Zoo. Indeed, it has been estimated that the number of people who see the lions and tigers at the National Zoo each year is greater than the entire visitor capacity of all the lion and tiger reserves in India.

For many years the zoo was the leading broker of a particularly spectacular strain of Bengal tiger—the white tiger—but in 1977 these were dispersed to other zoos. Part of the rationale was that because tigers are endangered in the wild, it was a better use of excellent breeding facilities and experience to build up captive populations similar to wild strains. The white Bengals were essentially an artifact of human breeding techniques. But nothing is simple: U.S. zoo populations of Bengals have in some cases been tainted with the genes of the whites. Similarly, some captive Asian lions have, according to sophisticated blood tests, been tainted by African lions. It is, in the words of one zoo curator, "something of a mess."

Now one white tiger is back at the zoo for exhibit purposes, and current breeding efforts at the National Zoo center on the much en-

(Left) These lions cubs, born in the zoo, are just beginning to lose the spotted coats they were born with. Soon their fur will be the uniformly tawny color of adults.

(Right) Perhaps a field mouse committed the fatal mistake of straying into a big cat enclosure: Something has caught this tiger's attention and he appears intent on snaring it. Mice and pigeons move in with most zoo residents, but rarely do you find a pigeon among the cats.

54

dangered Sumatran tigers. The wheels-within-wheels nature of the modern zoo's multiple concerns can be illustrated by the strategy developed for the Sumatrans. To avoid inbreeding, the young must be separated when they approach breeding age. But once separated, they tend to behave more like adults. On the other hand, with today's more sophisticated veterinary techniques, a young female can be implanted with a contraceptive device. Temporarily fixed, the female will continue to act more like a boisterous (and crowd-pleasing) cub and inbreeding will be avoided. Thus the breeding cycle can be managed to the advantage of the species and, to a degree, the zoo-going public.

Another popular stop at the zoo is the Ape House. It doesn't take much thought to understand why: the gap between ape and man is so narrow that one is forgiven the feeling of being not so much in the presence of beasts but merely seeing a different culture, mysterious perhaps, as any exotic culture is, but ultimately comprehensible. And, indeed, in the last decade or so, scientists have made increasingly detailed field studies of natural ape societies, and the resulting insights have made life for captive apes more comfortable. Gone are the open cages with bars of yesteryear, replaced with more curvaceous enclosures, separated from the public by glass, with places to climb and scratch against, and places also to disappear for a nap. Providing leafy trees for the gorillas, for example, appears to be impractical, given their propensity to strip off the leaves, but beyond the rear of their enclosures are trees to give the appearance of a natural setting. More important is to provide the gorillas with a substrate (a fancy word for floor) similar to what they experience in nature. Studies have shown that much of a gorilla's day is spent looking for food. Nowadays, the gorillas' substrate is covered with hay and leafy branches brought in by various keepers and volunteers. Raisins and seeds are painstakingly hidden in the hay and leaves: the viewer can see the animals acting naturally, foraging, and the animals are entertaining themselves by doing what comes naturally—a far better solution for gorilla boredom than the provision of daily television fare (which is beneath the intelligence and certainly the dignity of an ape).

Any zoo situation poses obvious challenges, the chief of which is how to manipulate limited space to the best advantage, a major preoccupation of all zoo managers. As pointed out, the principles of Hagenbeck have led to enormous improvements in the life of zoo animals and the enjoyment of zoogoers. A perfect example is the zoo's Monkey Island, its most naturalistic exhibit, a place where a troop of Barbary macaques cavort and breed with astonishing success, separated from the public only by moats and glass and, in a few places, by electrified fence. High atop the hill of their island, the monkeys can slip out of the public eye at will, but otherwise they are as accessible to view as any wild population has ever been. They have quality space—now the guiding principle for the design of zoo exhibits. Note the words of one of the many school curricula the zoo provides for the local community, this one concerning the design of proper zoo exhibits: "Recent research has shown that it is not the quantity of space which is important to captive animals, but quality of space—whether their enclosures contain . . . specialized areas. For example, hippos need and benefit from regular access to water. . . . The addition of a pool is much more important than any increase in the absolute size of the hippo's enclosure. . . . Humans also need and appreciate a certain amount of complexity (quality) in their living areas as well. Furnishing a room with one's belongings gives it substance and warmth. If your bedroom had only a bed, a lamp, and a dresser, which would you rather do: Move to a bigger room, keeping the same furniture, or keep the same room but hang posters on the wall, lay a rug on the floor, and buy a bookshelf and a chair?"

In this sense, the animal's needs are not so different from our own. It is the zoo's job to find out what "posters," what "rug," and so forth that each species prefers. Common courtesy figures significantly in providing for a particular animal's space requirements. Most of us maintain a certain distance between ourselves and strangers—just how much varies from culture to culture. It has been shown that in some cultures people will put their faces very close together when conversing, even with a stranger. For a northern European, such closeness would be uncomfortable, perhaps even threatening. Similarly, animal species have different amounts of space called flight distances that they naturally prefer to put between themselves and humans. Zoo exhibits nowadays try to keep this in mind, providing room in the enclosed area where the animal can stand as far from the visitors as it feels necessary. Thanks to this, the visitor to the zoo may often be largely ignored by the animals. Even a gorilla sitting just on the opposite side of the glass may pay no attention to onlookers at all. Here, just as with any exotic culture, it is advisable to recognize the local customs. Gorillas, for example, take it as a threat if someone stares directly into their eyes. The proper way to approach one of these animals is to get down on its level—by squatting on one's heels or bending over—and look at it only glancingly, preferably from over one's shoulder. Careful observation of the apes will show that this is how they communicate among themselves, and by adopting these habits, one may occasionally find oneself in a very pleasant communal moment, bridging an uncanny gap.

Gorillas at the zoo may simply dislike individual visitors. One youthful female orangutan has a definite preference for men with beards and will often gaze into such a blessed person's eyes with what appears, satisfyingly, to be adoration. A good way to see interesting human-animal interactions is to observe the keepers as they make their rounds. For example, when Lisa Stevens passes by the cages where some spider monkeys live, she will stick out her chin and the monkeys will respond in kind—their form of greeting.

Keepers and curators alike are constantly alert for information about the animals in their care, information that will enable them to provide optimum accommodations. One sign of an acceptable environment is activity. Inside the Monkey House, itself an old-fashioned building, one is normally greeted with about the same level of busyness as a playground during recess. In former days, it was customary to remove the young from the parents' enclosure once they were weaned. It has since become clear that among virtually all primates, as well as many other animals, it is important to keep family groups

Native to high rocky outcrops in North Africa and on Gibraltar, Barbary macaques (previous page) prefer high perches offering an unobstructed view of their surroundings. To accommodate this, the zoo built Monkey Island to simulate the macaques' natural habitat. A cooling waterfall cascades down the rocks, and the pool that forms the island gives the macaques a quiet place to reflect.

together for longer periods so that the young can learn the ways of parenting. Thus the cages in the Monkey House have large groups cavorting about on branches and sticks supplied by the keepers.

In this regard, at the turn of the century, most zoos tried to display as many different species as possible—often merely a pair of a given species. For example, in 1911, this same Monkey House displayed sixty-one monkeys representing twenty-five species. Now visitors will find fewer animals—about forty-five—representing only eight species. This philosophy of exhibiting more individuals of fewer species began in the 1960s and is now observable in the displays of virtually any animal that in nature is sociable. From the standpoint of the visitor, it is far more enjoyable to see a few bunches of animals being sociable than a lot of pairs looking lonely.

For most monkeys, the provision of more naturalistic settings is terribly expensive, they being adept at defoliation. It might be preferable, nonetheless, especially from the stand of the zoogoer, to see a bit of jungle in the enclosure. But would it be better for the animals? Beck says it would be fairly easy to determine if the monkeys prefer leafy branches over PVC pipe, but no one has actually researched the question. Conventional wisdom suggests that the Galápagos tortoise, which spends about half his time in the shade, would be happier with a large area of shade in his enclosure, but no one has yet experimented. Such research questions are on the docket at the National Zoo.

What animals to display and how to display them are decisions of nearly endless complexity and dimension. Availability of both animals and space is of course paramount, but always overlain by the availability of funds. The Reptile House is an example. Erected in 1929, this old building was the only space available when Dale Marcellini became curator of reptiles in 1979. No major overhaul, no new building was possible. A rectangular structure with display areas of mostly the same size running uniformly along both sides of the halls, with a few larger exhibit spaces at the narrow ends, the architecture presents something of a straightjacket, an old-fashioned museum atmosphere. Marcellini, with a herpetologist's faith in the intrinsic excellence of "his" animals, decided to make the best of the building and transform it into "a kind of art gallery." Each exhibit would be "pretty, natural, a little picture of a natural masterpiece." He decided that the difficulty of maintaining plants—they need a lot of care and the animals can disappear in them—was worth it. As a result, the National Zoo's Reptile House has a greater variety of habitats than any other reptile exhibition in the United States.

Here one will spot an orchid miraculously open next to a tropical frog—two jewels. Down the hall, in a pond where a Napalese gavial lurks in the clear water, a tropical forest of fronds and leaves hangs from above. A butterfly and a gecko forage for their own food, while the gavial makes slow, sinister, toothy sideways sweeps, snapping up the goldfish it is fed once a week. Elsewhere, in its own junglelike pool, a Cuban crocodile lies quietly, occasionally opening its great jaws—for reasons not clear. Maybe, Marcellini says, it is to cool off,

Favorites with zoo visitors, great apes such as orangutans—especially youngsters—also enjoy the diversion visitors offer. But available to all of the zoo's great apes are secluded spots where these sensitive animals can find privacy.

or to attract birds to clean its teeth. Or maybe it is simply some form of crocodilian self-advertisement. In 1985 the Cubans bred and produced the first crocodiles hatched at the National Zoo—an event all the more welcome since their species is endangered in the wild.

Feeding some of the reptiles presents a few unusual dilemmas—the most unsettling for herpetologists is that some of the reptiles eat other reptiles in the wild. A king cobra, obtained from the Bronx Zoo some years back, was a snake eater, but the republican Marcellini did not like the idea of reptiles eating their own kind: "They are all equal," he says. So he and the keepers devised a mouse sausage wrapped in the shed skin of a blacksnake and perfumed it with a blacksnake's musk to habituate the cobra to eating rodents. Soon it was unnecessary to use the musk; subsequently, the shed skin was not needed either.

There are numerous reminders of how dangerous reptiles and amphibians can be. Among the amphibian jewels on display are the poison arrow frogs—they have been boiled by South Americans in earlier centuries to make poison for their arrows, a toxin not unlike that derived by Haitians from marine toads to produce zombies. Closer to home is a common corn snake with a small sign stuck in the substrate of his exhibition space. The sign simply says Keep Out.

Turnover of animals in the Reptile House used to be rapid—not so much a matter of mortality as a desire on the part of keepers and curators to deal with new herps. (Conversely, the Reptile House also contains the best example of long-term commitment to an animal. This is Pigface, the aptly named African soft-shell turtle who has achieved a half-century of life and is the oldest animal in the National Zoo. Undaunted by his seniority, he amuses himself with a standard basketball.) The new philosophy is to create a balance among the different types of reptiles and amphibians—snakes, lizards, turtles, frogs, toads, geckos, and so forth—and to keep them on hand for longer periods of time. This reflects the high priority the zoo places on breeding captive animals and conservation. On the principle that not even the Louvre can house all the great masterpieces of art, the Reptile House, like the rest of the zoo, seeks to showcase a few kinds of creatures under optimum conditions. It is a gallery of exotica—merely to count the various kinds of dewlaps, crests, and bumps on the male lizards or to contemplate the range of reptilian hues is a breathtaking lesson in zoological variety.

Downstairs in the Reptile House is the first attempt in any zoo to redress an oversight of overwhelming proportion. It is no surprise that the zoo's current director, Michael Robinson, noticed this oversight. As a specialist in the behavior of tropical spiders, Robinson noted that nowhere in the zoo was there space given to invertebrates, which make up by far most of the animals on earth.

The Invertebrate Exhibit is home to all manner of creatures without backbones. The walls are dark and the lights low to show off the inhabitants of its spectacular aquatic tanks. Brilliantly colored anemones bear an uncanny resemblance to sessile flowers, but can transport themselves by inching along on their muscular bases. Sponges are another group of plant look-alikes that find themselves in this company. Other tanks house exotic crustaceans and mollusks, all in the family

(Left) With its shimmering golden halo and bright red throat pouch, an East African crowned crane captures the admiring attention of all passersby.

(Above) In parade fashion, turtles leave their pool to bask in the sun.

(Left) In winter, the zoo's resident waterfowl share their pond with migrating wild ducks and geese.

(Right) Large fish-eating water birds, double-crested cormorants dive underwater to capture their prey. Cormorants swim submerged up to their necks, then perch in the sun to dry out their feathers.

of what we commonly think of as seafood.

One of the most fascinating creatures here is the cuttlefish. A close relative of octopuses and squids, it has an amazing gift of camouflage. Its skin is full of color-filled cells called chromatophores. Expanding and contracting different combinations of these cells causes color change. When all of the chromatophores are contracted they allow an underlayer of cells to reflect and refract light so that the cuttlefish blends in with its environment. The cuttlefish uses these color changes not only to protect itself but also to communicate with others of its kind. Sometimes visitors are able to see these seemingly magical color changes if they happen to "eavesdrop" on a cuttlefish conversation.

Of course, there are plenty of insects and spiders hanging (and crawling) around. Some spiders are even allowed free range throughout the building; although they do tend to prefer the exhibit space designed for them, unlike their adventurous neighbors, the ants. Robert Hoage, director of public affairs, tells how the resident colony of ants escaped from their glass-enclosed home and found a drain in the floor nearby. They must have recognized a great opportunity because they began diligently carrying refuse from their enclosure down the wall and across the floor to the drain where they dropped it through the holes. A keeper traced their trail and discovered their clever waste management system.

A hands-on philosophy is paramount at the Invertebrate Exhibit, which is equipped with plenty of microscopes so visitors can examine the animals that live in common backyard soil. The walls have been cut away from the keepers' workroom to afford the public a view of what goes on to keep these animals healthy and their living spaces clean.

The zoo's efforts to familiarize people with the value and virtues of invertebrates are arriving none too early. Human destruction of habitats, particularly rain forests, is increasingly becoming a health hazard for these animals. Species of tropical insects are dying out before they are ever catalogued by scientists. Invertebrates are our most important competitors for the earth's food and active agents in the pollination of plants and the decomposition of organic matter. They are themselves the primary foodstuff for many species, such as the golden lion tamarins. Hearty and incredibly numerous, these small wonders deserve our notice and our respect.

In another "art gallery," presided over by William Xanten, is the most complete focus on small mammals anywhere in American zoos. One of the guiding principles in the Small Mammal House is to mix things up in a naturalistic setting. Xanten wanted to see different species in the same display; he wanted terrestrial and arboreal species together; he even wanted to throw in some amenable birds, like hoopoes and exotic starlings. He wanted to show arid, temperate, and tropical habitats. He wanted a high reproduction rate—despite knowing that if his small mammals bred too successfully, he might have a difficult time placing the extra offspring since few other zoos have much of a facility for these less-known masterpieces among mammals. He wanted to use natural plantings and naturalistic substrates.

(Left) Developing young can be seen in the translucent eggs of a long-armed octopus, one of the more spectacular creatures in the zoo's new Invertebrate Exhibit.

(Below) Truly a jewel among snakes, an emerald tree boa may coil—undetectable to human eyes—among the lush green foliage its color has evolved to mimic.

(Above) Generally active only at night, a pair of beavers makes a rare daytime appearance in Beaver Valley.

(Below) In this simulated rain forest in the Small Mammal House, a ring-tailed mongoose—one of the only pair outside of its native Madagascar—pauses for a moment before resuming its characteristic frenetic activity.

(Right) Oblivious to observers, a pair of Aldabra tortoises mates—a slow, protracted process in these lumbering reptiles.

(Above) Looking more like a log than a living creature, a Cuban crocodile lies mostly submerged in the murky water.

(Right) Hauled out on their rocky zoo beach, female California sea lions pose in the sun.

All he needed was a budget of about $250,000 — there wasn't one. So he asked for $20,000 for materials and some help from other keepers. For eighteen months, on their free time, keepers from all areas of the zoo, aided by volunteers from the graphics department, helped design and build all the new exhibits in the Small Mammal House.

"Artificial plants," he says, "looked terrible." Instead they used real plants, learning that if they installed toxic ones, the animals would munch the leaves "more judiciously." He found which creatures could live together: the acouchi and degu share food amicably, he says, but it's more a matter of individuals, he suspects, than any special compatibility between the two species. "It was something of a comedy of errors," he says, but nonetheless came up with three species of Asian squirrels that didn't fight among themselves. No mammal chauvinist, he installed some marine toads, not to produce zombies but to control mice. "They had little impact."

The dwarf mongoose, it was decided, should have a replica of a termite mount, that being the kind of neighborhood where these animals prefer to hang out. It took forever, Xanten recalls, to perfect the termite mount. The keepers had to learn how to dribble wet cement and then paint it to look accurate. Since then, starting with a single pair of dwarf mongooses, Xanten has had a phenomenal breeding success and is constantly scrambling to find other zoos where the excess can go. On the other hand, the ring-tailed mongooses are the only ones in captivity outside of their native Madagascar and they have not mated. Artificial insemination is under consideration.

Most of the animals in this area are diurnal. The keepers stagger the feeding times of them all so that the visitor has a good chance of seeing these interesting, if often overlooked (and even mispronounced), animals being active. It is enticing enough to know that if one is lucky, Xanten says, one might see an elephant shrew dancing on the back of a plated lizard.

Each area of the National Zoo has its own personality, its own mood. The colorful beauty of the reptiles is matched only by the dazzling denizens of the Bird House — another place of natural settings reproduced in this case behind cleverly arranged walls of almost invisible wires, permitting subtle intimacy. In the vast outdoor flight cage of fine mesh, a design that itself suggests flight, the imagination soars with the free-flying inhabitants. Down in Beaver Valley, where bears of various kinds lumber about on their own business and otters ply their watery slide with ottery abandonment and the sleek seals preen in the afternoon sun and one occasionally hears the most pristine of sounds — the howl of a timberwolf — it is possible to be in the Far North and think with awe and perhaps some sadness about the great wilderness of North America now so shrunken. The zoo is a park, an island of sanity in a shrinking world. It is, as a popular slogan has it, the wildest place in town. It is a place to come and mingle with strangers, to enjoy the exuberance of children amazed, a place in which to be reminded of the wonderful diversity and inventiveness and beauty of life and to reflect on how precious, how awesome, how delightful all of life is.

BEHIND THE SCENES

The National Zoo has been compared to a city, to an ecosystem, to many other organizations, but no such metaphor withstands scrutiny. There is simply nothing else that is like a zoo, and there is no other zoo like the National Zoo. Three million people a year visit and absorb what is there to be seen. But most of what transpires in the zoo is not on public view. Indeed, much of the rest of this book is devoted to the multifarious activities of animal maintenance, health care, conservation, and research both here and abroad. But before looking behind the scenes, it is time to consider another of the zoo's collections—one that by some ways of calculating dollar value may well be worth more money than the animal collection: trees.

When a former director, Theodore Reed, hired a young horticulturalist named Richard Hider in 1979, he explained: "This is the National Zoological Park, not the National Zoological Gardens." He meant that the emphasis should be on trees, not flower gardens. The parklike effect of large shade trees is as much a part of the zoo's ambience as the howls of the gibbons or the playfulness of the seals. Indeed, the original design of the zoo was by Frederick Law Olmsted, the designer of New York's Central Park, perhaps the most famous and revered park designer in United States history. In fact, Olmsted's original designs for the park have been mislaid along the way, and much of the park has grown in ways that could not have been foreseen at the turn of the century. The new Olmsted Walk that snakes

Towering above even the tallest giraffe, trees native to the eastern deciduous forest, as well as Asian and European imports, give the National Zoo its pastoral ambience. Set within Rock Creek Park, one of the world's largest urban national parks, the zoo's 167 acres provide a refuge from the fast-paced city that surrounds it. Perhaps famed landscape architect Frederick Law Olmsted (shown below in the light suit) envisioned Washington's future development when he surveyed the site of the proposed zoo, which in 1889 was still "out in the country." Olmsted's plans preserved the landscape's natural features: steep-sided ravines on the sides of a long sloping ridge following a great bend in Rock Creek.

curvaceously through the zoo, tying the exhibits together, is a deliberate return, with the help of local Olmsted scholars, to what has been reconstructed of his plan. But for years, the trees have stood as direct effects of the Olmsted legacy. There is, in some parts of the park, a bit of a "monoculture," Hider says, of red oak and tulip poplar, but a computer survey in one quadrant of the zoo, completed with the help of interns, showed ninety-four different species. While the zoo is nothing like the National Arboretum across town (yet), a tree-fancier will find one hundred trees labeled, and Hider plans more along with a scheme to produce detailed tree management histories for most of the large ones. Besides Hider's managing and replenishing the zoo's trees, his other task is to landscape exhibits. In this kind of zoo horticulture, Hider says "we're flying blind." There have been great zoo horticulturalists, but they have rarely recorded what they have learned. Furthermore, Hider says, every animal is different and will react differently to plants in its enclosure. "My job is to try to stay one step ahead of the animals." Often, he doesn't. He grins widely as he explains how he put three large honey locust trees behind hot wires in the African elephant, Nancy's, yard. One day she charged the electric wire support frame, ripping it out of the ground. On the advice of the collection manager, the wire barrier was removed. Nancy promptly ate the tree and the dirtball. "It made a very interesting exhibit," he says, "for a few minutes."

Everything at the zoo turns into science before long. Hider is trying to plant American chestnuts here and there. He is using seedlings that have been bombarded with radiation in an attempt to alter their genes sufficiently to make them resistant to the chestnut blight—one of the zoo's lesser-known efforts on behalf of endangered species.

Rarely does a horticulturalist smile at the memory of a devastated tree, but of course, at the zoo, the daily and long-term needs of the animals come first, even for a botanist.

On the edge of one of the lower parking lots, there is a building that is not unlike the concrete bunkers along Atlantic beaches from which the Coast Guard kept an eye out for German shock troops. Most of the building is buried in the hill. Down on one of its lower floors is perhaps Washington's most unusual and largest kitchen. This is the zoo's commissary, presided over by Moses Benson, who came to the zoo as a keeper in 1960. All new keepers at that time worked for thirty days in the commissary (then located in the basement of the Reptile House) and Benson liked the work. Except for a nine-month stint with the lions and tigers, he's been in the commissary ever since. Today he manages an annual grocery budget of over $500,000 and mountains of garden variety and exotic foods. By six in the morning, the commissary is something of a madhouse.

At that time each day, four stewards and a foreman have begun to load tons of food onto waiting trucks, some of it, like Zupreem Special Marmoset Diet, is esoteric; and some of it, like Uncle Ben's Rice, is familiar to any frequenter of supermarkets. Although the people food makes one feel at home, the atmosphere overall is as exotic as the Monkey House. A man in arctic wear opens a vast metal door, and an enormous cloud of moisture emerges like a polar giant's breath.

The ceiling inside is festooned with stalactites of frost. It is twenty-five below in this room that holds vast quantities of meat, bread, fish, and rats. Everything is larger than life. There is a room full of baby food, like Gerber's, and dried milk and formula. One shelf holds enough wheat germ oil to supply a health food store for several months. Gallons of peanut butter and what seems to be a lifetime supply of shiny red delicious apples are also stashed in the commissary.

Each week the grocery lists are submitted by the keepers from the various animal groups. Moses Benson and his staff organize the food according to each group's order (unfreezing meat, for example, and running it through the giant mixer along with other prescribed ingredients, such as special minerals and vitamins). The next morning, the orders are loaded up to be delivered to their destinations.

Some of the delicacies on the commissary menu seem to fall short of mass market appeal, such as Zupreem Diet, though Benson pointed out once that as primates we could survive for quite a while on nothing but cans of Zupreem. (It is full of healthful things like wheat germ, and one probably could survive on it, though it has a slightly cloying sweetness to it that would become tiresome after a day or two.) These special foods are contracted to suppliers and make up a relatively small fraction of the commissary's annual budget. Twice a year the ingredients are analyzed in a laboratory at the zoo to make sure they remain up to the zoo's precise specifications.

It all makes perfectly good sense, this commissary, once one considers the clientele. The giant pandas love the red delicious apples. The bats need a special vitamin fortification. It's natural enough to order gallons of salad oil for the zoo because it is used not for a salad but for lubricating the elephants' dry skin. Part of the clientele is insectivorous, so Benson purchases, along with mealworms by the pound, some thirty-eight thousand crickets a week from such places as the Cricket Farm in Baton Rouge. It seems, upon reflection, perfectly straightforward that there are cricket farms. But a visitor remains stunned by the sheer quantities here. The mind reels, almost panics, at the thought of that many crickets.

Every Thursday a huge truck pulls up to the loading dock and eight thousand bags of herbivore diet are loaded aboard to supplement the diets of the animals at the zoo's Conservation and Research Center in Front Royal, Virginia. Only a big-time farmer can truly understand that. Benson himself grew up on a farm. It is common, he says, for zoo people to have come from farm families. Such people, he suggests, often possess what he considers a prerequisite—a sense of humor.

One can get an overall sense of life in the commissary from a typical week's food order chosen at random—in this case, Morna Holden's request from the Elephant House: 98 pounds of apples, 56 pounds of bananas, 35 loaves of bread, 42 eggs, 175 pounds of kale, 42 pounds of oranges, 56 pounds of potatoes, a case of honey, two cans of applesauce, a case of dry cereal, a case of evaporated milk, several cans of vitamin and mineral supplement, several bags of special diet pellets, a bag of wheat bran, four bags of oats, and (in the hope-springs-eternal department) one case of Mumm Champagne, Brut.

Feeding nearly 7,000 animals of about 450 different species—each with its own special nutritional requirements, the zoo's commissary caters to more diverse tastes than any restaurateur could imagine. Some menu items, however, appeal to many of the zoo's animals. Fresh fruit and vegetables, zoo "bread" baked fresh in the commissary (left), live crickets (top), or newborn mice and rats form all or part of the diets of many zoo residents from frogs, lizards, and snakes to birds and most mammals. Fish of various kinds comprise another widely appreciated entree and are the mainstay of seals and sea lions. Each day a California sea lion eats about fifteen pounds of fish and a gray seal up to twenty-five.

(Next pages) Like other felids, lions use their four large canines to grab and kill prey—even if the "prey" is a zoo-provided shank bone (top)—and premolars or carnassial teeth with sharp cutting edges to shear meat off bones (center). With jaws capable only of vertical movement, lions are unable to chew; massive jaw muscles, however, exert a powerful gripping force (bottom). Anticipating his morning meal of meat and bones, a tiger (right) tries to monitor the activity of keepers who prepare and deliver his food. Never fed on exhibit, tigers readily return to their indoor enclosures at mealtimes.

77

Even without such celebratory items, these shipments are anxiously awaited. Of an early morning outside the Lion House, a tiger sits expectantly at the door, as aware of the time of day as anyone wearing a watch. Inside the keeper is preparing the food for the big cats. Along with fruit, vegetables, and cereal, the four tigers and lions consume thirteen expired chicks a week, 240 pounds of special feline diet, and 450 pounds of meat. As often as not this is the meat of nutria (technically the hair is called nutria and the animal a coypu). The nutria is a beaverlike, semiaquatic animal of South America that has been introduced into North America where it has thrived. The big cats' nutria are from special breeding farms: for this purpose the animals are simply ground up. "You find teeth and other stuff," says the keeper over a special din, a sound peculiar to the intimate basement area of the Lion House at feeding time. Even a seasoned keeper can be forgiven for starting slightly at the abrupt, guttural snarl of a tiger impatient for breakfast. Then the keeper calmly drops a trayful of nutria meat through a specially engineered opening in the wire mesh cage, and it is attacked by the world's most accomplished trencherman with low growls of aristocratic pleasure. Four hundred pounds of rib and shank bones from a horse are provided each week to keep those big teeth in dental trim, says the keeper as she approaches the enclosure of Zike, a male Asian lion who instead of coming forward to get breakfast is nervously pawing at an empty beer keg, clutching it to him suspiciously. "This one won't mate, so far," the keeper says. "He was brought up with only males before we got him in 1985. We gave him that keg for amusement and now it's like his blanket. He'll probably get over it."

Once aware that his keg is safe, the lion proceeds to devour his rations with gusto, an activity that never fails to strike one as elemental . . . the simple act of ingesting ground nutria meat becomes, in these jaws, an awesome, splendid, terrifying spectacle, the quintessential carnivorous business.

Such classifications are sometimes tricky. The giant panda is classified as a carnivore, but it subsists in the wild as well as in the zoo on a diet chiefly of bamboo. Ling-Ling and Hsing-Hsing's diet is supplemented by a number of other vegetables and fruits, but they will be carnivorous and eat any mice they catch among those that scuttle about in their enclosure. (For this reason, pest controllers cannot put out mouse poison but must settle for less efficient traps which, in a fine circle, is why there are mice in the Panda House. At the zoo virtually everything is connected.)

Working out the specifics of diet for the zoo's three or four thousand animals is ultimately the responsibility of Olav Oftedal who in 1979 became the first full-time zoo nutritionist in the United States, entering a field where virtually everything is discovered by trial and error. Oftedal is impelled by an ocean of ignorance about the diet and nutritional needs of exotic animals. With a small staff, he is engaged in asking simple questions. Thirty-eight thousand crickets are ingested at the zoo in a week? What nutrients are found in a cricket? Is the cricket's exoskeleton itself nutritious or mere packag-

ing? What's in bat's milk? Seal's milk?

Feeding is thus one of Oftedal's preoccupations, and each species in the zoo presents a slightly different set of requirements. "Most animals," Oftedal says, "can adapt quite handily to poor food—food that lacks a lot of the nutrients they would normally get in the wild—so long as nobody is expecting them to reproduce or their young to grow."

The young of monkeys that are folivorous, or leaf-eating, need fiber. How can that be best introduced into their diet? How do they handle tannins and other toxins often present in leaves? Insect-eating creatures need calcium. Can crickets be fed a diet rich in calcium, and then pass it along? (The answer, it turned out, was yes.) These are the questions daily addressed in the nutrition lab, where gleaming equipment like infrared spectrometers is used to do mineral analysis, fat level counts, protein and nitrogen determinations—a regular assay of what goes in and goes out—in order to reproduce in captivity the optimum counterpart to what is ingested in wild nature. Oftedal's program of applied (and sometimes basic) research is the first of its kind in the country. It is conducted in cooperation with numerous universities and other agencies, often taking researchers into remote and dangerous places. The University of Miami, for example, will ship Oftedal's lab a batch of milk samples from dolphins, killer whales, and manatees for needed analysis. In the other direction, the zoo will call on others to help supply information.

Gary Alt of the Pennsylvania Game Commission is the leading expert on black bears and has worked with Oftedal in studying cub nutrition. The zoo was interested because it was thought that black bears might make a reasonable analog for giant pandas. In more than ten years working with black bears, Alt has even successfully intro-

A hooded seal pup nurses for only four days—less time than any other mammal—before being weaned and abandoned by its mother. In this short time, however, a pup doubles its weight, growing from about forty-five pounds at birth to ninety pounds at weaning.

duced orphaned cubs to new mothers. Having found that a potential foster mother would reject cubs as surely as a skin graft, Alt determined that the rejection was based primarily on smell—the new ones smelled wrong—so he short-circuited that message by the simple expedient of daubing the foster mother's nose with Vicks VapoRub.

What struck Oftedal as fascinating about the black bear was that cubs are born during the somnolent time of hibernation—a time when the mother neither eats, drinks, nor eliminates wastes, and a time when it is near freezing even in the den. Close observation showed that the cubs will scream like bloody murder if they become detached from the mother and her circle of warmth. The noise is sufficient for her to "awake" enough to pull the cubs to her again. While her physiological processes are damped, she nonetheless lactates. Additionally, black bears are widely hunted in Pennsylvania. There is a brief hunting season of two days during which hunters eliminate twenty percent of the population. This ratio, which could be fatal for some species, does not endanger the black bear population because they are very productive breeders, averaging three cubs per litter, and because the cubs grow very fast—even as their mothers are physiologically "out of it" in many ways. For the milk-oriented nutritionist, this anomaly deserved attention.

Black bears are, according to Alt, relatively docile. He found one once perfectly happily denned in a tree a few feet away from a residential mailbox (the homeowner was unaware of the bear's presence). If a black bear comes at you, Oftedal reports, "you just wave your arms and she'll stop and go away." Nonetheless, to intervene in a bear's den is almost by definition a parlous practice, so to look into mother-offspring relations requires that the hibernating mother be darted with anesthetic. Then she and her cubs can be safely weighed and examined at various intervals.

The joint investigation has shown that the mother's milk production is identical to her weight loss during hibernation—approximately thirty percent of her body weight. Efforts are now underway to find out how much fat the mother loses, a measure of the energy drain from feeding the cubs. And of course all these measures of loss are to be compared to measures of the cub's gain. Thus a practical question—what should be fed to a baby panda if it needs human help—leads to basic questions about bears in general.

Even more exotic and more intrinsically irresistible to a fellow who might be called the Milk Man was the case of the hooded seal. The zoo had a long history of interest in seals and seal lactation, having dispatched researcher Daryl Boness and others to explore the matter among various species. The period from birth to weaning for seals is short compared to most mammals. But hooded seals, which give birth to pups on the arctic pack ice just as it is about to break up with the onset of spring, seemed to have an unusually short lactation period: it was thought to be about two weeks. Oftedal and Boness joined with the Canadian Department of Fisheries and Oceans in 1985 to research this hypothesis.

Having located the herd from the air, they set out on the Canadian research vessel, the C.S.S. *Baffin*, in league with two helicopters, and tagged and marked the newborn pups. Long-range radio transmitters placed on the ice permitted the researchers to return to the site each day through the cloud cover and fog. Each pup was checked to see if it was still suckling, still gaining weight, and still had milk in its stomach. When the answer to all of these questions was no, the pups were considered weaned. (The seal mothers evidently didn't mind all this manipulation of their offspring, but would merely sit idly by while it took place.)

Oftedal speaks with awe of the results of this study. The pups weighed forty-five pounds on average at birth. They achieved ninety pounds at the end of four days, at which point they were weaned. This is the shortest lactation period of any species of mammal known, and probably the greatest rate of growth. It is almost possible to observe the growth directly. The mother seal's milk is about sixty percent fat, lab analysis has shown, compared to forty percent for whipping cream. In this surge of productivity, the hooded seal mother is computed at providing some sixty thousand calories a day, enough to feed about twenty-five humans. And practically nothing is wasted: a plug of fur and feces serves to keep the milk in the pup where almost all of it converts to blubber. What's the rush? Why this believe-it-or-not race to feed baby hooded seals? Little is known of the overall ecology of this species. The scientists hypothesize that the birth is delayed by the fact that hooded seals' food supplies are not abundant in the calving grounds so the mothers must feed for a long time to build up the fat reserves they need. Thus birth occurs at the point when the pack ice is breaking up, victim of storms and warmer weather. The pups have to wean quickly to be on their own when the ice is gone. Also, young seals are subject to predation by polar bears. If the period from birth to weaning is short and takes place when the ice is at its weakest, this danger is largely eliminated.

The practical applications of this research are yet to be felt at the zoo, where the daily necessities of looking into the digestive physiology of red pandas or comparing the diets of iguanas in Panama with those in the zoo take precedence, but it is likely that this extreme case will, in due course, help save a life. Such thoughts are of course too melodramatic to appear in scientific papers, as are the events that surround such research in faraway places. But to a curious visitor, Oftedal will dwell a bit on the adventure involved, characteristically downplaying his derring-do. It seems that after the research was accomplished on the hooded seals and the scientists were leaving, one of the helicopters failed as it was flying out of Saint Anthony, Newfoundland. Oftedal and several others were stranded on a lonely rock at sea, and as night fell, they confronted minus thirty-degree temperatures and strong winds. There was little else than a few low, wind-blasted trees on this rocky island. Using the only tool available—Oftedal's Swiss army knife—they managed to cut a few branches to start a fire. Huddled around it throughout the night, with their parkas suffering only a few burns, they lasted until morning when they were finally rescued. Zoo work is rarely routine.

Good nutrition is, quite obviously, a major component in the maintenance of health among the zoo's inhabitants, and one less obvious

Regular collection and analysis of blood samples from birds and mammals, annual physical examinations of gorillas and other primates, and closeup monitoring, often via video camera, of newborn young and their mothers form part of the zoo's aggressive preventive medicine program. These procedures supplement the health information keepers glean daily from careful observation of their charges.

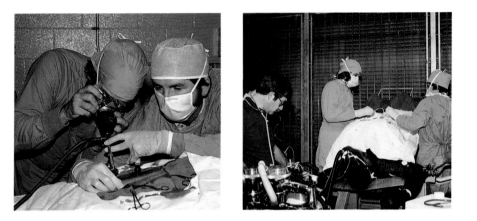

aspect of nutrition is the quantity of food an animal eats. Sometimes there are mild disagreements about this. Administratively, a curator manages all aspects of a particular collection. The keepers report to a curator. But cutting horizontally through such vertical management lines are the people from the Office of Nutrition and those from the Office of Animal Health—the veterinarians. Ideally, they all collaborate to develop a complete regimen by which a given animal will be maintained, but zoo people tend (beneath all the organizational charts) to be a bit free-spirited. Keepers, being closest to the animals in their care, often feel that they know what is best. And indeed they often do. But, as Benjamin Beck explains, with a tolerant grin, some things are a little hard to control. "For example," he says, "the big cats don't have to hunt for a living in the zoo. So they miss out on some exercise they'd normally get, and they tend to get a bit overweight. So we will decide every now and then that the big cats should fast for a few days. But the keepers—well, they're like anxious mothers, you know. So they might keep a stash of bones on hand so the cats won't feel altogether miserable during fast days." He shrugs. "Things usually work out pretty well."

All of the zoo's animals receive state-of-the-art veterinary care to ensure their health and comfort throughout their lives.

While the health of the animals is everyone's business, it is the only business of the Department of Animal Health, presided over since 1972 by a veterinarian named Mitchell Bush, who has upheld the tradition of his predecessors to make the zoo preeminent in the field of health care for exotic animals (the previous director, Theodore Reed, was trained as a veterinarian).

The delivery of health care has come of age at the zoo with the completion of two hospitals, one on the zoo's Rock Creek Park grounds in Washington and one at the Conservation Research Center at Front Royal, Virginia. The hospitals are equipped to meet the needs of their patients, which is why the state-of-the-art hydraulic surgery tables can handle animals weighing a ton or more. Both hospitals use a computer system to keep detailed records of the medical history of each animal in the zoo's collection.

Bush and his staff spend long hours providing and overseeing preventive health care. The first line of defense against disease is the quarantine ward, located in a separate building from the hospital. All newly acquired animals spend their first days in this ward where they are tested for infectious diseases that could endanger other animals or keepers and are given the necessary vaccinations. Most animals remain here under observation for about thirty days.

Once animals have joined the collection, they are constantly monitored for disease and nutritional problems. Daily vigilance is critical because many animals mask any symptoms of illness. In the wild, a sign of illness or weakness will quickly gain the attention of a sharp-eyed predator; zoo veterinarians depend on another sharp eye—that of the keeper. Through daily familiarity, keepers can spot an unfamiliar behavior, be it a change in posture or eating habit, or even a different smell associated with the animal. In addition to the keepers' observations, preventive health care includes regular checking of stools for parasites and periodic blood tests and physical examinations. Primates, for example, receive an annual physical comparable to those humans get.

The veterinarians, of course, are treating unwilling and often dangerous patients. So manipulative procedures like physical exams, blood sampling, and bandage changes require some sort of anesthesia for the safety of both doctor and patient. The Department of Animal Health performs about 1,400 anesthetic procedures a year, and these result in reams of data useful not only to the zoo but also to other veterinarians dealing with exotic animals. The zoo staff chooses to use anesthesia to minimize stress and allow a more complete examination of the animals.

Each species can provide a separate range of difficulties. Take the giraffe—the choir of biologists do not sing the same tune about the basic physiological processes by which a giraffe pumps blood against gravity all the way to its lofty head, or why it doesn't faint when it raises its head after a drink of water. Anesthetizing one thus presents a dramatic series of challenges, not the least of which is that if a giraffe collapses abruptly, it can severely injure itself or the people working with it. The zoo veterinarians have developed a protocol of anesthesia that calls for sedating the animal to the point where it can be handled (for such routine matters as a blood test), then fully anesthetizing it in the down position. Once the giraffe is down, its heart and breathing are carefully monitored because CPR for these large patients is impossible. Reversing these steps is a still more delicate operation. If the giraffe returns to consciousness too quickly, it will thrash around to regain its feet and injure itself or the anesthetist. So a protocol has been developed for administering a series of drugs to control the animal's arousal from anesthesia.

In general, many diseases seen in zoo animals are comparable to those seen in their domestic counterparts. Thus, the zoo veterinarians often encounter familiar diseases in unfamiliar species and have to extrapolate from the training they received with domestic species. Many bird problems are comparable to those found in domestic chickens; similarly with canids and felids. Such carnivores as raccoons and badgers have diseases common to both dog and cat; most hoofed stock will display problems found in cattle. Zebras, rhinos, and, to some extent, elephants can be compared in terms of disease and basic physiology to horses. As more is learned about exotic species, how-

Zoo veterinarians pioneered techniques for immobilizing high-risk exotic animals like giraffes so they can be safely examined or treated for disease. A sudden collapse will often prove fatal to a giraffe, as will letting its head and neck fall to the ground (right). In an immobilization procedure, veterinarians first enter the enclosure of a lightly sedated giraffe to string two tiers of rope across the cage and to place a rope halter around the giraffe's head and neck (top). They use the halter to lead the animal so its upper and lower neck leans against the ropes, which then catch the giraffe as it falls into deeper anesthesia, allowing them to slowly lower the giraffe's head (middle). All the while the giraffe is down, they monitor its heartbeat and other vital signs (bottom), prepared on a moment's notice to administer drugs to reverse the anesthesia should the giraffe show signs of distress.

ever, this kind of extrapolation becomes less necessary. Zoo veterinarians are laying the groundwork for the new field now called zoological medicine.

The veterinarians have many years of practical experience in zoological medicine and receive questions daily from colleagues at other zoos. Even if a problem is unique, someone on the staff can usually provide insight derived from similar cases or from intuition developed over the years. It is by no means a one-way street. Zoo veterinarians these days are part of a regular network of information exchange on zoological puzzles.

Recurring medical problems in the zoo population drive the department's research program. One current study involves the treatment and control of shigellosis, a bacterial infection that affects primates. Gibbons are especially vulnerable to the disease, but even humans can catch it. The zoo is testing an antibiotic that eliminates the disease in the carrier state, an effort that will help primate collections worldwide, but also people living in developing countries who may be exposed to the disease. Much research by zoo veterinarians is conducted on animals in natural habitats since their physical condition provides insight into the problems of captive animals. A recent field study involved administering tuberculin tests to elephants in the wild to help researchers understand why elephants and other nondomestic hoofed stock have false positive reactions to the test.

These days Bush and his staff see more and more of a new health concern for zoos—geriatrics. Geriatric problems include tumors, heart disease, and old-age organ failure—strangely, a good sign that the zoo's maintenance of its collection is successful. Unfortunately, geriatric medicine will never be as effective in zoo patients as in humans or domestic pets, says Bush, because it requires a large degree of patient cooperation.

Naturally enough, in spite of great strides in animal health care delivery, there is an annual attrition rate of fourteen percent. Even this is turned to advantage. No zoo animal dies without going to the Department of Pathology, one of only a few zoo pathology programs in the United States. Richard Montali runs this operation, which handles not only autopsies but also complete laboratory tests, such as blood analysis, interpretation of biopsies, and other diagnostic evaluations.

Blood analysis is particularly complicated because each species has unique forms of red and white blood cells and a unique total blood count. Now technologists at the Department of Pathology can recognize what is normal or abnormal blood for most species in the collection, but it took years of examining many blood samples. An animal's blood is tested during sickness, during its annual physical, and during quarantine coming or leaving the zoo. Often these blood tests uncover hidden illnesses. For example, liver damage was discovered in the red pandas during a routine blood test and traced to dietary factors. Now that the diet has been corrected, the red pandas have perfectly healthy livers.

Diagnostic work in the Department of Pathology has enabled the zoo to prevent epidemics of diseases that have threatened the collection over the years. Duck viral hepatitis, a fatal herpes virus infection

Immobilization makes possible the safe transport of large animals like gorillas (below), procedures such as the artificial insemination of a giant panda (above right), and the treatment of such routine health problems as overgrown hooves in zebra and other ungulates (below right).

found in waterfowl, and canine parvovirus, a disease of domestic dogs, are two diseases of free-living animals that have infected the zoo's population but, fortunately, have been diagnosed and brought under control before they became widespread.

Thanks to the rigorous testing that goes on here, any giant pandas that may be born have a set of antibodies waiting for them. Montali determined that newborn pandas were dying of infections because their immune resistance was inadequate, so he arranged to have antibodies extracted from the parents' blood to transfer to the next baby panda born. It was also the work of Montali and his staff that identified congenital hernias and cockroach-transmitted parasites in some of the golden lion tamarins: those affected were not allowed to be part of the outward bound program.

After death an animal is given the most thorough examination. Part of each organ is preserved and made into microscopic slides that are closely inspected to determine whether any damage was incurred by disease or injury. Cells from tissues removed during an autopsy are cultured in the lab and then frozen at a temperature that stops their growth but does not kill them. Thus, many zoo animals are outlived by their tissues. These frozen cells can be used for research, reducing the need to take tissue samples from live animals for studies. All of the details this intensive probing yields are entered into a computer, so information on any disease or any species can be retrieved instantly.

Birth, weaning, health, disease, death are daily events in this exotic island in the capital city's midst, and like much of the business of Washington, the zoo's affairs are tended behind the scenes by people whose names never appear in headlines. Here the heroes are the animals on display and only the antics of a few are noted in the local press: the anxiety that surrounds the breeding of the giant pandas, the birth of a giraffe, the passing of a favorite big cat, the arrival of a new gorilla. But every such event in the life of even the "lowliest" of zoo creatures is chronicled with a nearly biblical fervor, winding up ultimately in the records of Judith Block, the registrar, whose goal is to track everything important in the zoo.

"At any one time," says Block, "we aren't keeping very many animals. To learn anything, you need long-term data." The data she manages are part of a tradition that stretches back to the 1890s when the zoo was founded as part of the Smithsonian Institution, where the museum-bred tradition of tracking every accession is part of the culture. Every incoming animal, every birth, even every stillbirth gets a number, thus "creating a record." Every loan agreement, permit, export, import, and exchange is handled and recorded in the registrar's office, along with age, sex, parentage, and change of enclosure. Even "parts and products" are documented: for example, blood samples taken from tamarins released in Brazil are shipped to the zoo for analysis and became part of the record. Every bird egg that pips gets a number and becomes part of history.

Some statistical compromises are made. It is one thing to see that no sparrow falls without a record, but amphibians have simply too profligate a reproductive system for every tadpole to be recorded. In-

What sets zoos apart from other kinds of museums is that the specimens in zoo collections die. But at the National Zoo, even a sad death becomes an opportunity to learn more about how to care for the animals in its collection. Every animal that dies in the zoo undergoes a necropsy—the animal equivalent of a human autopsy—to determine the cause of its death. Information obtained from necropsy is then used to improve diagnosis and treatment of diseases and other health problems of living animals. However, to bring a dead animal to the zoo's pathology building for necropsy is not always easy: A crane had to be employed to move a greater one-horned rhino that died in its enclosure.

stead, a rule of thumb is used to estimate the production of eggs and a standard percentage is used to derive the number of tadpoles.

Keeping track of adults is a tricky business in some instances. Keepers are encouraged to sketch the patterns of snakes through time and successive molts to be sure they are talking about the same one in all cases. Even larger creatures must be tagged or tattooed: with the skepticism of the born record keeper, Block tells of instances when field biologists, who claim to be able to recognize individuals in a herd or group simply by their individual markings, were asked to differentiate between members of the Père David's deer herd at the zoo and got it wrong.

No one, however, who works for long in a zoo believes the possibility of perfection, and one of Block's favorite stories is at her own expense. At the outset of 1973, the year after the giant pandas had arrived with unprecedented fanfare, the director gave her a call after reviewing the annual year-end census. He simply wanted to point out that the inventory looked just fine except for one thing: the pandas weren't listed.

Is such a seemingly fanatical care for record keeping mere icing on the cake? Not when one realizes that it is precisely such records kept only at the National Zoo and a few others that made possible the central revolutions in zoos in this century. The ramifications of the direct results of the record keeper's craft are main threads through the remainder of this book.

Accession No.	Scientific Name	Common Name	Sex	Locality	From Whom Received	When Received	How Acquired	Remarks
						1961		
					Police Lt. Col. S. Sikhumvat 31 Soi Pasang Ekamai Rd., Bangkok Thailand			
28,80*	ANASTOMUS LAMELLIGERUS	Open-billed stork				Nov. 11	Purch	
	MICROHIERAX CINERBICEPS	Feilden's falconet	♀		" "	Nov. 11	Purch	
	TESTUDO EMYS	Mountain tortoise			" "	Nov. 11	Purch	"Six legged tortoise"
	VARANUS DUMERILI	Demeril's monitor			" "	Nov. 11	Purch	
28,81	GEKKO GECKO	Tokay gecko			" "	Nov. 11	Purch	(Released in crocodile cage)
	MALACLEMYS TERRAPIN	Diamond-back terrapin			Mrs. Agnes Caddington 900 Notley Road Silver Spring Md.	Nov. 12	Gift	
	GLAUCOMYS VOLANS	Flying squirrel			Mr. Lee Gray 1700 N. Tyalor St. Arlington Va.	Nov. 13	Gift	
	PANTHERA LEO	Male lion			Philadelphia Zoo Philadelphia Pa.	Nov. 14		To be shipped to British Guiana Shipped 12/1/61
	CTENOSAURA ACANTHURA	Spiny-tailed iguana				Nov. 17	Exch	
	BOA CANINA	Emerald tree boa				Nov. 17	Exch	for 2 yellow-necked parrots
		Ragon-billed toucanets				Nov. 17	Exch	
	Alligator mississipiensis	American alligator			Dr. Martin Cline N.I.H., Bethesda	Nov. 17	Gift	
	DEIROCHELYS RETICULARIS	Chicken turtle			Tote-em-In Zoo Wilmington N.C.	Nov. 18	Exch	
	ELAPHE QUADRIVITTATA	Chicken snake				Nov. 18	Exch	
28,82	BISON BISON	American bison	♂♀		San Antonio Zoo San Antonio Tex	Nov. 19		To be shipped to India
	MACACA PHILIPPINENSIS X M. IRUS	Hybrid macaque				Nov. 20	Born	
	COENOBITA CLYPEATUS	Hermit crab			Mrs. Pearl Jacobs	Nov. 21	Gift	
	ELAPHE QUATUORLINEATA	Four-lined snake			Tote-em-In Zoo Wilmington N.C.	Nov. 22	Purch	
	Leptodeira annulata	Cat-eyed snake				Nov. 22	Purch	
	PECARI TAJACU	Collared peccary	♂			Nov. 23	Born	
	BUTEO PLATYPTERUS	Broad-winged hawk			Tr. A. S. Mosby Wildlife Unit Blacksburg, Va.	Nov. 23	Gift	
	POTOROUS SP.	Rat kangaroo				Dec. 1	Born	First observed in pouch
	UROLONCHA DOMESTICA	Bengalee finch			Mrs. Inez Latham 716 Kearney St. N.E. D.C.	Dec. 8	Gift	
	AMADINA FASCIATA	Cut-throat finch			" "	Dec. 8	Gift	
28,83*	AIDEMOSYNE MALABARICA	Indian silver-bill				Dec. 8	Gift	

91

OVER IN A MEADOW

Mainlining testosterone, the male deer sets forth up the hill away from the wet bottomland where his misty-eyed harem waits passively. He has already adorned his brown back with mud, having tossed it there with a flick of a second-rate set of antlers. Partway up the slope, he horns the ground again, flinging more mud and festooning his rack with tufts of long dead grass.

In a stiff, mechanical gait, he marches upward, head down. Below his eyes are dark streaks—preorbital glands now open, giving his visage even from afar a look of maniacal if goofy determination. The male is all business, driven by a chemical imperative. His abdomen is tucked up anorexically: he has eaten nothing during the several days of his tour of duty, a nearly constant frenzy of patrol, paranoia, and procreation.

He strides on, dead grass swaying from his antlers like Spanish moss, an awesome if temporary embodiment of single-minded, macho. He is a Père David's stag, and he is operating in as wild and free an environment as any of his kind have enjoyed in two millennia.

Such creatures, we are assured, cannot do arithmetic, but the stag has somehow sensed a problem, a flaw however perceived in the perfect hegemony he seeks to exert over his world. Far above him in a meadow a female languishes dreamily, and some fifty yards beyond her, lingering near a tree, is a svelte male, sleek and elegant in his antlerian symmetry.

(Previous page) On the rolling hills of the western slope of the Blue Ridge, Père David's deer live much as they might in their native China had they not been extinct there.

(From left to right) Antlers adorned with tangled strands of grass, a rutting male Père David's deer looks for a chance to gain control of a herd of females. Meanwhile, a current harem master, similarly decorated, stands firm among his females, then approaches one in a posture called a "low stretch." This female tries to escape the male's attention, but her erect tail indicates that she is in estrous. Such scenes are common during the rutting season, which extends from May to September at the National Zoo's Conservation and Research Center at Front Royal, Virginia.

The harem-master of the moment advances deliberately toward the female. She looks up and, chastened, trots quickly back down the hill to rejoin the harem, still lolling placidly on the marshy ground. The stag, stiff-legged, advances a few steps closer to the interloper, who turns away and moves into the trees. The old stag follows the errant female. He emits a long low roar, the sort of sound one might expect from a misshapen foghorn, and for the moment all is well.

Before too many days pass, the stag will be unceremoniously replaced by another—in fact, his fall from the heights will be accompanied by certain ancient rites, notably predictable events arising from a more determined aggressiveness on the part of some other male, perhaps the one biding his time up the hill. The current stag has been in charge now for a week or so and his predecessor, bruised and sore, is about a half a mile away, alone in a fenced enclosure.

The herd's home is on the steep, rounded slopes of the Blue Ridge Mountains in Virginia in the National Zoo's Conservation and Research Center. The route by which these deer arrived in this altogether improbable habitat began in China, and it is only thanks to the intervention of a nineteenth-century French missionary and several generations of dukes of Bedford, among others, that they are here at all.

The European mind became aware of these deer only in the late nineteenth century when a Catholic missionary with an abiding interest in natural history sallied forth from France to China as part of the European attempt to make the mysterious Middle Kingdom safe for civilization. Père Armand David was stationed in China from 1862 to 1874, where he moonlighted for the National Museum of Natural History in Paris while engaged in the business of saving souls. In the latter work, he was not especially successful, even discouraged by what he took to be Chinese spiritual intransigence, but perhaps his heart was not altogether in it. He once had written: "I passionately love the beauties of nature; the marvels of the hand of God transport me with such admiration that in comparison the finest work of man seems only trivial."

In three expeditions in search of the beauties of Chinese nature, David managed to send back a host of plant and animal specimens then unknown to Western science, including the first giant panda. In his travels, he came across an animal called the milu, now known as Père David's deer. Even then it was not found in the wild, but instead only in the imperial hunting park near Beijing. This deer was an early victim of habitat destruction, most of its natural environment along the rivers of China having been turned to farmland in early history. Indeed, records suggest that the milu had existed only in parks at the sufferance of Chinese nobility since the time of Christ.

Although it was forbidden to enter the emperor's game park, Père David was able to obtain several skins and some antlers and send

Most Père David's deer births occur in the late spring, by which time males have shed and regrown their antlers in preparation for the summer rut. Typical of polygamous species, males provide no care for young.

them to Paris, where a new species was recorded: *Elaphurus davidianus*. A century later the largest single herd of these animals roamed Woburn Abbey in England, the estate of the duke of Bedford, with other scattered groups here and there in American and European zoos. Today, the second largest collection is at Front Royal, inhabiting some seventy-five acres, where the ancient rituals embodied in the species' DNA are still played out in an environment that strikes a neophyte to zoos as oddly permissive. The displaced stag convalescing in a separate enclosure far from the harem was, even to an unpracticed eye, in considerable discomfort—a condition zoo people generally spend their waking hours assiduously trying to eliminate. But here, at Front Royal, animal husbandry and its associated travails—while monitored with nearly voyeuristic precision—are allowed to take a somewhat more natural course than is possible in the restricted area and atmosphere of a zoo.

To the extent that competition between males leads, in nature, to the best genes being passed along, so it should be in the quasi-natural environment of the Front Royal center. Controlled competition is allowed, and in their first ten years at Front Royal, the Père David's deer gave birth to more than one hundred young, many of whom have been shipped selectively and with the usual care for sound genealogy to other zoos. There is something a bit melancholy in the thought that this species has existed in the shadowy area between the wild state and domestication for nearly two thousand years and that that will continue to be its fate for the foreseeable future. On the other hand, consider the alternative.

That alternative—namely, extinction—is the main reason there are zoo people at Front Royal, an hour and a half by car from the National Zoo in Washington. The center consists of 3,150 acres of mixed pasture land and woods near the northern terminus of the famous Skyline Drive that runs north and south along the Blue Ridge Mountains. The Appalachian Trail maintains an easement on the center's southern boundary, and local streams plunge down steep hillsides into the Shenandoah River, which winds past the nearby town of Front Royal. Enclosed and crisscrossed by forty miles of chain link fence, the center is not in gentle rolling foothills one associates with the romance of Virginia: these hills soar and plummet, with an altitude change of five hundred feet, giving the vista a breathtaking verticality. People driving below in the valley along Virginia Route 522 are often astounded to see a small herd of antelope with long curved horns on the greensward above the highway. Indeed, it is averred that a particular curve on Route 522, where the center first becomes visible, bears more burned rubber than any other stretch of road in the county, the sort of unscientific rustic datum that calls for no corroboration.

Nestled among the hills of the center is what appears from a distance to be a self-contained community—one clearly of military origin: a cluster of buildings with red-tiled roofs and walls painted the color of manila folders. For years, the center was a remount station for the U.S. Cavalry, a place of barracks, stables, barns, and trim homes for officers and NCOs. Near an old track, one can still visit the graves of the officers' favorite horses and pet dogs. In 1948, sometime

Their antlers still partly covered with velvet, two males not yet in rut graze peacefully in the lush spring grass.

Dirt roads provide the only access to the center's far-flung pastures where Burchell's zebra and other exotic species live and breed in relatively natural circumstances.

after tanks replaced horses as the preferred steeds of blitz-minded armies, the center became a beef cattle research station of the United States Department of Agriculture. Then, in 1970, the USDA decided to close it down. The procedure for disposing of such federal lands is to give other agencies of the government first crack, and when Edward Rivinus, then with the Smithsonian Secretariat, saw the routine announcement, it took only a few days before the Smithsonian pounced.

It was becoming evident to people in the zoo world at that time that zoos might well end up as the only home for various species of animals—temporarily, at least, until the steady erosion of wild habitat was reversed. But if zoos were to become arks, in this sense, they required a great deal more than forty square cubits of space.

Edward Rivinus, sitting in the Castle where the Smithsonian's administration operates, knew well of Theodore Reed's goals in this regard, and within days the zoo, first among several other government agencies, had staked its claim on the old remount station. With a temporary permit and just a little of the spirit of the buccaneer, Reed immediately began moving animals out to Front Royal to take the wind out of the sails of any other potential applicants; in 1975 the National Zoo officially became 3,150 acres larger. That same year Christen Wemmer, a specialist in ungulates and carnivores who had worked at Chicago's Brookfield Zoo, was appointed curator-in-charge of the center at Front Royal.

Less than a decade and a half later, the Conservation and Research

Center had become a major arena for the husbandry of exotic creatures—visibly dominant among them ten kinds of hoofed stock, but including eight other mammals and twenty-one species of birds. The place seethes with sex and reproduction. Formerly, the center housed one of the largest incubation and rearing operations outside of the poultry business, with thousands of eggs laid by birds both at the Center and at the zoo in Washington, giving rise to hordes of chicks tagged and catalogued with the precision of a fine library and, in most cases, hand-reared. Although the spring still brings an annual egg frenzy for curator of birds, Scott Derrickson, and the seven keepers who care for the resident bird collection, there have been marked changes in the propagation operation in recent years. As Derrickson notes, "We have deliberately reduced the number of species in our collection, while increasing the number of individuals per species; a process that has improved our animal management and husbandry standards, as well as our research productivity. Each year breeding objectives are established for each species in the collection at the center and at the zoo in Washington, and we focus all of our efforts on achieving these specific goals. Our emphasis has generally moved from one of quantity via hand rearing to one of quality via parent rearing."

Among the most unavoidably noticeable of the birds are the cranes, some rare, others less so, but all truly exotic in their form—the giraffes of the bird world. Looking northward from one of the high hills of the center back toward the cluster of buildings, an entire southwest-facing hillside is seen to be covered with wire mesh, a bit like a shantytown suburb of the old remount station's central city. Here one finds the hardier birds, mostly pheasants and cranes that can, with the help of radiant heat panels, withstand the icy cold of the Front Royal winter. Like any shantytown, it tends to be noisy, although in this case it is often the wild, trumpeting calls of the cranes that pierce the quiet of the place.

Moseying along the road past these hardy bird enclosures, one may be glared at by an elegant white-and-black bird that stands nearly six feet tall, a red-crowned crane, of a size to dominate even the whooping crane. Not nearly as endangered as its North American cousin, the red-crowned crane of Asia nevertheless now numbers only about one thousand in the wild. The bird is represented at Front Royal by a mere eight specimens, including four that were hatched and parent-raised at the center.

Meanwhile a larger flock of a related and nearly as endangered bird, the white-naped crane, also of Asia, has produced eighteen young under the guidance of Guy Greenwell, the former curator of birds, and Derrickson, who had worked with whoopers at the U.S. Fish and Wildlife Service, Patuxent Wildlife Research Center in Laurel, Maryland, before joining the National Zoo.

Both the white-naped crane and the red-crowned crane are included in cooperative Species Survival Plan programs, in which captive populations are genetically and demographically managed under the auspices of the American Association of Zoological Parks and Aquariums and its foreign counterparts. As of 1989, fifty programs had been es-

The Conservation and Research Center's first exotic residents were one male and two female scimitar-horned oryx which formed the nucleus of its first breeding program. Once ranging throughout the semideserts of North Africa, this large antelope is extinct north of the Sahara, and endangered in its last strongholds in the Sahel. But the herd-living oryx thrives in the spacious pastures of the center where more than one hundred calves have been born since the breeding program began. Both males and females display the long, scimitar-shaped horns that give this species its common name. Horns may be used to defend access to the scarce food and water resources of the oryx's natural habitat.

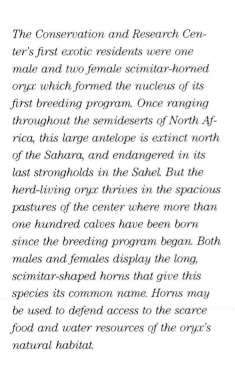

tablished for endangered species in need of intensive captive breeding. This program is detailed in the next chapter, but suffice it to say that Species Survival Plans, involving the active cooperation of many zoos on behalf of such species, are certainly at the heart of the new zoo.

Cranes are tricky to breed. As is so often the case with species in trouble, little is known of their habits and preferences. Part of the program for developing breeding techniques for these rare birds is the use of surrogate species for research and observation. At Front Royal, pairs of Stanley, sarus, and sandhill cranes were maintained for years under rigorously monitored conditions for just this purpose. Except for a few pairs of sandhills still remaining at the center, all of these birds have been transferred to other facilities so that available space can be devoted to the rarer red-crowned and white-naped cranes.

Similarly, the North American black ducks are being maintained and produced at the center to be used in investigating the effects of in-breeding and developing reintroduction techniques. Such information, it is hoped, will be readily transferable to other endangered species such as the white-winged wood duck, a native of Southeast Asia, where deforestation and warfare have ravaged its habitat and left a mere two hundred pairs in the wild.

Two bird species from Guam—the Guam rail and the Micronesian kingfisher—have become a major focus for the National Zoo and are under Derrickson's care at the center. The problems began in the late 1940s when the brown tree snake was inadvertently introduced to the island. As so often happens with species that are accidentally or deliberately introduced into wholly new habitats, the tree snake found little natural opposition in the form of predators, so its population steadily grew. By the early 1980s the snake had eliminated several endemic forest birds and left many others in immediate danger of extinction. In cooperation with Guam's Division of Aquatic and Wildlife Resources, the Philadelphia, Bronx, and National zoos launched a major effort to save the island's native avifauna. Unfortunately, by the time this rescue effort was initiated, only three species—the rail, the kingfisher, and the Marianas crow—remained in sufficient numbers for captive propagation. Both the Guam rail and the Micronesian kingfisher are now being bred successfully in a number of U.S. zoos, including the center and the zoo in Washington. A captive breeding program for the crow is next. As with the golden lion tamarins in Brazil, the plan is to reintroduce these species to the wild once the tree snake has been brought under control.

In obtaining Front Royal, the National Zoo was annexing no perfect Eden, no tabula rasa upon which to inscribe the perfect breeding grounds for the world's endangered wildlife. There were, initially, the eternal limitations of budget appropriations. The center remains strained in terms of human resources (there is a ratio of one keeper for thirty-eight mammals, which is about as far as a keeper can go). There was the preexisting limitation of architecture. Enclosures of an average size of thirty acres could be built by the tedious installation of mile after mile of chain link fence with gates within gates. Barns could be refurbished, stables and even dormitories converted into indoor en-

Double-wattled cassowaries are New Guinea's largest land animals. Bred at the center, this young cassowary will become independent of its father after about one year. Males in this species incubate eggs and raise chicks with no help from females.

Two sarus cranes born at Front Royal. In years past, this species served as surrogate for other, endangered species of cranes, allowing center staff to learn, using a common species, how to breed rare ones. Not very prolific breeders, most cranes produce only two young a year.

closures for birds and mammals. And there was the altogether inexorable matter of the seasons, which range from nearly subtropical in Virginia's summer to glacially cold on its windswept mountains in winter.

The ability to withstand the seasonal fluctuations of the weather played a considerable role in the choice of animals that could be housed at Front Royal. For this reason, work with tropical exotics had to be restricted to the Great (actually Cramped) Indoors—a severe handicap to the center's flexibility. In some cases enclosures were built both inside and outside of the existing building, thereby allowing animals to be appropriately housed whatever the weather. Several buildings were modified in this fashion for housing the Rothschild's mynah, a beautiful white starling relative from the Indonesian island of Bali. This bird, also known as the Bali mynah, is one of the great success stories. It was nearly extinct in the wild when it arrived at the center in 1976. Now more than two hundred young have been hatched at Front Royal, and a vigorous, cooperative Species Survival Plan program is underway in North American zoos. In 1987 a number of mynahs were transferred from the center and other U.S. zoos to the Surabaya Zoo in Indonesia to establish a captive breeding and reintroduction program. Several young hatched at the Surabaya Zoo from these birds have already been released into the wild in the Bali Bharat National Park, nourishing the hope that this program can ultimately save this elegant species from extinction.

The Small Animal Facility has begun to loosen the climatic restriction. Opened in 1983, it contains spacious indoor enclosures similar to those typical of new zoo installations, linked with equally spacious outdoor enclosures. Here shrill, energetic golden lion tamarins share the corridor with placid tree kangaroos but can comfortably avoid contact with humans.

Along with the tamarins and tree kangaroos is a handful of handsome, little-known (in this country), and wholly misnamed mammals called tiger cats. They are neither tigerish, nor catlike. They are spotted, not striped. They are capable of a scream akin to a buzzsaw, though not a roar. They resemble a marten more than anything else but have also been compared to an opossum, which is closer because tiger cats are marsupials, mammals with pouches in which the fetal young develop—perhaps a more ancient reproductive strategy for mammals than the placental scheme. With a few New World exceptions like the opossums, marsupials are Australasian creatures that in the course of evolution radiated in form and function to fill virtually every niche available. Thus there are carnivorous marsupials, leaf-eating marsupials, mountain-dwelling marsupials and prairie-dwelling marsupials. Marsupials are proportionately more endangered than their placental counterparts.

The tiger cat, or the tiger quoll (rhymes with ball and derives from an aboriginal name for the animal), may well have struck early explorers as analogous to a pole cat. Where the tiger reference arose—perhaps from its outlandish scream—is questionable. In January 1984 two female and two male tiger quolls were obtained from the Tasmanian

(Left) This Rhea chick is one of many born at Front Royal. These large flightless birds are native to South America's pampas grasslands.

(Above) Stanley cranes, native to central Africa, were once bred at the center and are now on exhibit at the zoo.

107

Thanks to a successful breeding program, zoo-born Bali mynas are being returned to Indonesia, where fewer than sixty wild mynas remain in a small reserve on the island of Bali.

National Park and Wildlife Service and installed in the Small Animal Facility. They were under the care of Larry Collins, curator of mammals at the center. Collins was a specialist in marsupials before taking charge of Ling-Ling and Hsing-Hsing in 1972. When the Front Royal center became a possibility, Collins was among the first to head west. He scoffs at the label marsupial expert. ("There's no such thing," he says. "We only started looking at marsupial behavior seriously in the last ten years.") But one senses an especial delight on Collins's part with the tiger quolls and, in particular, a female named Stella. Stella became the first of her kind to raise young outside of native tiger quoll habitat.

There was a seasonal consideration from the start. Tiger quolls were known to breed during the austral winter, probably activity keyed to the shortened photoperiod of winter days. Would these animals adjust to the topsy-turvy seasons of the northern hemisphere? In the fall of 1984 the quolls' keepers began running them together in pairs—Stella drawing a male named Angus, the other pair being Melbourne and Sydney. The urban pair showed little interest in each other, but Stella and Angus were observed mating in early December. Yet inspection of Stella's pouch showed no result in mid-January (the gestation period for these animals was thought to be about three weeks). The couple was put together again and more mating took place over a four-day period. By February, Stella greeted Angus with the sound of a circular saw, so he was confined elsewhere, and when Stella's keepers noticed that she was making nest-building motions, they began fattening her up lest a hungry carnivorous mother eventually find plump joeys too tempting. In early April, two joeys were indeed spotted in her pouch. She was given almost total privacy, the keepers swallowing the urge to inspect the joeys, and the mother spending the greater part of her days in a hole she had excavated under her nest box.

Within a month the little family was free-ranging throughout the enclosure, with the young becoming increasingly agile and independent, learning rapidly to catch crickets supplied for their nutrition and education, racing in joyous circles about the enclosures, and climbing on the branches overhead. Not until August when the young were fully weaned from Stella did their keepers attempt to catch them to determine their gender. Both females, they were named Alice and Adelaide, and the center, ever expansionary, hoped to obtain two more wild-caught males to pair with them in due course. Now, after years of breeding, the tiger quolls appear to have joined their neighbors in the Small Animal Facility, the tree kangaroos, as marsupials whose lineages seem secure in captivity.

Asked about this success and others that adorn the center's record of breeding exotics, Collins explained, "Basically, we just set 'em up in nice quarters and leave 'em the hell alone."

Naturally, it is more complex than that. Much is won by a quasi-parental empathy that one finds almost uniformly among zoo people. A small breeding victory is to be found in the modified corncribs across the road from the Small Animal Facility where one sees red pandas lounging on shelves and branches, unquestionably among the most appealing of animals anywhere in the world. Unconcerned by the continuing discussion in certain scientific echelons about how closely related evolutionarily red pandas are to giant pandas—less related now than they were a few years ago—keepers at the center have experienced a red panda baby boom. Some of this success must be attributed to the introduction of specially designed concrete nest boxes into the enclosures in 1984. The breeding mothers had seemed uncomfortable before: the boxes supply a cool place for the animals to raise their young during the hot summer months, this species being a highly seasonal breeder and a cold-climate animal.

One program thought to have ended in disappointment was recently revived. In 1984 the black-footed ferret presented itself as an ideal candidate for the Front Royal treatment. The only known population of these weasel relatives was located near Meeteetse, Wyoming, in an area of short-grass prairie. A plague among the prairie dogs that make up ninety percent of the ferrets' diet seriously threatened the species. The Wyoming Game and Fish Department, along with the U.S. Fish and Wildlife Service, recommended establishing a captive population while intense efforts were made to eradicate the plague. Collins and Curator-in-Charge Christen Wemmer duly filled out a species acquisition proposal. A year's experience in the 1960s at the U.S. Fish and Wildlife Service's Patuxent Wildlife Research Center suggested that captive ferrets would accept small mammals other than prairie dogs as food, needed to be housed separately, being solitary creatures, and needed a minimum of disturbance and a natural (dirt) substrate—all conditions easily met at Front Royal. The species acquisition form was sent to Director Michael Robinson, who found the proposal exciting and appropriate, as did the other twenty-eight members of the zoo's Animal Programs staff to whom the proposal was circulated. Sadly, the young ferrets caught after the 1985 breeding season had distemper. End of project, at least temporarily.

The Wyoming Game and Fish Department was eventually able to rescue through distemper immunization eighteen black-footed ferrets before the Meeteetse population dwindled to nothing. The small group that saved the species produced seven young in 1987 and thirty-four young in 1988. In the fall of 1988 four female and three male ferrets were delivered to Front Royal in a National Guard cargo plane from the Wyoming Game and Fish Department's Sybille Wildlife Research and Conservation Education Unit.

Valiant breeding efforts are not always sufficient to save a species. These ferrets at Front Royal, born and raised in captivity, need to learn survival skills if they are ever to be reintroduced to the wild. The zoo is currently using a surrogate species, the Siberian ferret, to test instructional materials, including a stuffed great horned owl suspended on a monofilament line and a stuffed badger, called the robo-badger by some, mounted on a remote control miniature automobile frame. Confrontations with the robo-badger and the owl are supposed to teach the ferrets how to recognize and respond to actual predators. The method has proven effective in other captive-raised endangered species.

For now the ferret story has a happy ending, but as Wemmer cau-

Pairs of exotic cranes live in a row of large, fenced enclosures, each with its own heated shelter, while many native birds make their own homes in the center's fields and forest.

(Following page) When an abundant white-tailed deer population began to overbrowse the center's forest, wild deer had to be excluded with a special deer-proof fence.

tions, "A zoo, a place like this can only address a fraction of what is going on. We need thousands of places like this. Even then, we're bound to lose a lot. You can overstate the case for what zoos can do: the most important thing zoos can do is educate the public. We don't deceive ourselves about what we're doing here. We have to be realistic. We may just be recording bits and pieces of information about things that are going to disappear."

Why bother? Wemmer talks of growing up in San Francisco, at fourteen years old part of a student science group at the California Academy of Sciences, collecting reptiles and amphibians.

"My father told me I couldn't make a living by playing with animals. But I've always had a fascination for wildlife, and here I am making a living by 'playing with animals.' Most conservation-minded people are to some degree romantics, and so am I. We're doing important things here."

Against the urgency and the awesome odds, the usual atmosphere at the center is nonetheless one of overall calm, the steady purposefulness one sees on most farms. It is, of course, a pastoral place, its purpose to provide "nice quarters" where matters can take their course. Driving here and there in an open jeep with Larry Collins as he takes his occasional patrols of the ungulate herds, hopping out time after time to do gate duty, one is lulled into a sense of bucolic peace as Collins slowly passes grazing onagers and oryx in pastures enclosed by chain link on his way to a precipitous descent down a pasture to a knoll where a herd of sable antelope graze. The unhurried pace, the relaxed attitude, is belied only by the beeper radio on Collins's belt, by which he stays in contact with the center's support people, reporting such trivia as a too noisy humidifier in the Small Animal Facility.

The sable antelopes perceive little disaster in the oncoming jeep: they turn their white-streaked faces toward the interlopers—a row of saturnine African masks—and then casually move away a few feet.

"They're skittish," Collins says. "The vet was just in here, trimming their hooves. Every now and then you've got to trim their hooves. Give them a good diet and a soft pasture and their hooves don't wear down."

Seeming more bored than skittish, a dark form slowly gets to its feet, a recently arrived two-year-old male from the zoo in Omaha. Elsewhere, higher up in another enclosure, is another herd under the sway of an old male named Diablo—a jet-black old warrior with but one horn, a dangerous-looking reason to believe in unicorns. This male, the sleek, heavily muscled young Nebraskan, turns his back to the jeep.

Most of the center's female sables came from the National Zoo and the New York Zoological Society's St. Catherine's Island, the results of two relatively common bloodlines: this explains the presence of the new male who, at two, may be a bit young to breed. But Collins is sanguine.

"The English," he says, "tell us that sable antelope breed only at three years of age, but we've had a yearling breed here. Maybe it's

something in the grass." He leans over the wheel of the jeep for a moment in simple admiration. It all seems perfectly natural, sitting near this herd of antelope, lately from the heart of darkness, now munching grass on the slopes of the Blue Ridge foothills as cumulus clouds billow up in the west. For a moment, the foreignness of the animals and the unfortunate reasons why they must be here are lost to daydreams.

Not for long. Returning from the high ground to the cluster of buildings below, the jeep passes a long stretch of fence consisting of high tension wires, constructed to lean outward away from the wire mesh enclosures. The intent is to keep out white-tailed deer, a multifaceted plague at the center.

Local deer learn early that the grass is greener inside the center's perimeter. They leap the fences or lurk patiently alongside Route 522 waiting to follow cars through the gate. In a place like the Front Royal center deer can be lethal. Some are host to brainworm, which in a few instances has infected the center's wildlife, resulting in the loss of six reindeer and two sable.

In the early 1980s, the center became the eye of a storm of controversy when, overrun with deer, it invited the Virginia Fish and Game Commission to oversee a controlled hunt to reduce the deer population. There ensued a blizzard of letters to local newspapers and the zoo, calling such a plan inhumane. Against the outrage, explanations were useless: opponents would not consider the relative value of a herd of endangered antelope compared to an unbridled population explosion of deer, the epidemiological danger of the deer; the fact that deer populations have been managed precisely through hunting by local and state authorities for decades, and the fact that the activity would put venison on the tables of local people who would hunt one place or another anyway. The plan was dropped, but the four-legged interlopers did not go away. A new fence, a New Zealand product discovered with the help of a Virginia sheepherder, was installed at some considerable cost to keep the deer off the watershed above the hoofstock yards, and the deer problem was ninety-nine percent under control—at least until the next population explosion.

Between natural pests and community relations, the officials at the center always have a number of things on their mind in addition to ex-

(Previous page) Several species, including the red panda, breed both at the center and at the zoo. The red panda breeding program is one of the National Zoo's most successful, with more births of this rare species than at any other zoo in the world. Native to high-altitude bamboo forests in central Asia, the red panda's status in the wild is uncertain, but its future in zoos seems secure.

Animal keepers at Front Royal proudly display a litter of squalling clouded leopards (left). These beautiful Southeast Asian cats proved difficult to breed in zoos until careful studies revealed that a male-female pair must be formed while both animals are still youngsters; allowed to grow up together, a male and female will ultimately produce young of their own. Virtually nothing is known about this shy cat's behavior in the wild.

The center's scientists are trying to devise ways to instill fear of predators in zoo-born black-footed ferrets (above) so this critically endangered species can be returned to the wild. (Below) This Siberian ferret, a surrogate for its black-footed cousin, is being trained to avoid a "robo-badger," a model for predators black-footed ferrets are likely to encounter on their native Great Plains.

otic animal husbandry. Deer are not the only natural pests: there are still a few large carnivores left in the mountains around Front Royal— bobcats, bears, and such. Their populations are sizable, but they do not cause the center much trouble. Groundhogs, however, can wreak havoc in pastureland. In burrowing under the fences, they provide ingress for raccoons and foxes, that prey on young birds and eggs. And any place with animals and animal feed will attract rats, mice, snakes, and cockroaches. Pest control at the center is in the hands of a Vietnam War veteran named Gary Holder. In Vietnam, Holder served as a supply officer, and from his office in the center's commissary he manages the annual importing of 15,000 pounds of fruit and vegetables, 5,000 eggs, 556,000 crickets, and 344,000 pounds of pelleted food, as well as the raising of 40,000 live mice and 750 rabbits. In a good year, Holder can predict the annual feed needs of the animals within two percent. A state-certified pest control expert, he favors insecticides that contain an otherwise harmless growth hormone. Cockroaches, for example, that ingest it grow to adulthood, the only effects being crinkled wings and sterility. One finds no cockroaches at the center. The battle against other vermin is ever more effective, though there is no record anywhere of such creatures surrendering unconditionally.

Local dogs are an occasional plague: dog owners rarely realize that once let loose, dogs revert to more ancient urges, especially in the company of others, forming vicious, if temporary, feral packs. Arthur Cooper, animal keeper foreman at the center, speaks feelingly about this particular problem. Cooper lives in a small stone house high on a hill near the southern end of the center and spends much of his free time walking around the perimeter fences. Often he will encounter dogs who have made their way through the fence and he will call them. When they come to him, Cooper (who used to manage the big cats at the zoo in Washington and has pictures of lions he hand-raised on the walls of his office at the center) will contact the owners or, failing that, take the dog to the pound.

Some intrusions make Cooper sad. Others make him angry. He tells of hunters trespassing to poach deer, and he clearly is worried about the poachers' ability to differentiate between a white-tailed deer and an oryx: "All those nuts running around with guns," he says, shaking his head. But he reserves his true wrath for the occasional vandalism. For example, people on three wheelers have destroyed fences and gates and blitzkrieged about the premises on misbegotten larks. Asked what his options are in such situations, Cooper again shakes his head and says, "Only to seek prosecutions."

These are some uncommon hazards in raising exotics in Virginia; another is fire. Once a welder let some sparks fly into the window frame of a barn near which he was working. Noticing this, he poured water on the frame; since there was no further smoke, he worked on and left. Later that night, the building burst into flames and was severely damaged before the blaze was extinguished. No animals were in it and the barn was rebuilt, but the event was an actual reminder of a specter that haunts people at the center—the possibility of losing animals to a fire. To this end the center has its own fire brigade and several volunteers are trained in fire prevention and control. In one

old garage in the cluster of buildings are two gleaming, properly bright red fire engines—both as bizarre in their own way as is the vista of sable antelopes on a Virginia hillside. One, a brush truck, was built out of a surplus army weapons carrier. The other is an ingenious home-grown contraption; the origin of which was a surplus 6 × 6 army fire truck. Like many of the exotics at the center, they have names: Li'l Bucket and Big Bucket. Big Bucket is the only ten-wheel fire truck in the county and has found a great deal of use as an auxiliary to the county's fire suppression system, helping out in difficult hollows and hills. Nor do the center's community relations stop at the edge of Warren County, Virginia. They extend, in a sense, throughout the world.

Each summer since 1981, the Front Royal center has hosted another kind of exotic group, at the specific invitation of Rasanayagam Rudran, the zoo's conservation program officer, a man with a quick smile who administers one of the most unusual schools anywhere in the world, the Wildlife Conservation and Management Training Program. For eight weeks each summer, Rudran is a professor, housefather, and cheerleader for some dozen and a half recruits from Africa, Asia, and South America, who gather to learn the hands-on techniques and principles of wildlife management. They are rapidly steeped in such technology as radio tracking and they plumb the mysteries of such mathematical matters as the minimum convex polygon.

The course is remarkably intense, for belying his soft voice and kindly dark eyes, Dr. Rudy (as the students come to call him) is a high-voltage man, a gentle revolutionary from Sri Lanka. He rarely relaxes during the course that normally takes place from early June to early August. He is a constant presence, prodding, explaining, as quick to ask a question of strategy, science, or philosophy as he is to smile—the gentle challenger. His students never return home—to China, Zambia, Venezuela, or wherever—thinking the same way they did before arriving in Dr. Rudy's all-purpose radio-tracking, vegetation-censusing, confidence-building crash course in wildlife management principles, respect for wild nature and human nature, political strategem, bureaucratic tactic, and the culinary arts.

"These people will have to be cooperating in the field right away,"

115

says Rudran. "They start in the kitchen. I break them up in teams and each team has to take responsibility on certain days for all the cooking and cleaning up. If they don't learn to cooperate, they don't eat. It's very effective." He smiles as he speaks, sitting at a table in a large room given over to a restaurant-style kitchen in the center's conference building. "The men from developing countries," he goes on, "usually have never been in a kitchen before. Even if they wanted to go in the kitchen the ladies wouldn't let them. Here, some become very good cooks."

Around the metal counters six members of the class, in a ballet of activity, have created a meal for seventeen people without a single spill or quarrel. Rudran turns his attention to a young man at the table. Unlike the others in the class, this man—from India—is not a biologist or biologist-to-be, but a journalist specializing in wildlife stories for Indian magazines and newspapers. Rudran had decided earlier, when the candidates for this year's class were being selected, that it would be worth dedicating a space to creating a more sophisticated wildlife journalist.

"You can't blame the system all of the time," says Rudran. The journalist had just spoken of the need to implement draconian legislation that calls for evicting some people and their cattle from the vicinity of a small sanctuary in his home state in India. Rudran had smiled and asked: "But can you sell conservation that way? If you move people away from their traditional homes, aren't you putting people through an awful lot of hardship?"

The journalist explains further: "But these are very rural people, very illiterate. It takes so long to reach them, to persuade them. And it is very politicized. The legislature says they must move, the tribal elders agree that they will all move, and agree that they must accept compensation to move, and the political opposition starts brushfires of disagreement and nobody moves . . . years later they are still there and their cattle still run in the sanctuary."

At this juncture Rudran cautions the young man not to ignore the needs of humans. The journalist continues undaunted.

"But these are very traditional people. Education is a very long-term process in India among such people. When things are urgent, some traditions must be broken down." He proceeds eloquently about how fragile the sanctuary is, how great the pressures on its survival.

"Yet," says Rudran so quietly that he can barely be heard over the clattering of dishes being washed in the metal sink, "if you force people to move, doesn't this mean that you are treating them the same way the colonials treated you? Maybe that's a tradition that should be broken too."

"But," the journalist remonstrates, with a nervous smile, sensing his own entrapment, "that is how it must be. The grass is always greener in the sanctuary so the people bring their cattle in. They must be told to move. We still have a feudal society and problems can be solved only from the top down. It has always been this way in India."

Rudran nods understandingly and leans forward. "One man can bring about change, you know. In your country there was a man named Mahatma Gandhi . . ."

The journalist ducks his head. "But a man of such energy as that, of such wisdom. . ."

"One man," says Rudran. "Anyone can make a start. The change has to start with someone. It has to come," he pauses and smiles, "from the bottom up." He tells a story.

As a college graduate in Sri Lanka, Rudran had landed a good and safe job in an oceanographic institution but heard that some zoologists from the Smithsonian Institution were soon to arrive to perform field studies on the elephants of Sri Lanka and other wildlife. Rudran told his father and his university professor that he was going to quit his job and volunteer to work for the Smithsonian scientists. Both of them discouraged him from giving up his security. He managed, nevertheless, to join the Smithsonian team, ending up later in the United States for a doctoral degree as well, then returning to Sri Lanka to perform a government-sponsored environmental impact assessment of a huge agricultural development project. Officially, he was reporting to a government agency, his only avenue for exerting any influence over the outcome of the assessment, which was specifically to determine the probable effects of development on an area of lowland tropical forest and its fauna.

He decided to explore another avenue of influence—the grassroots—and discussed strategy with some conservation-minded Sri Lankan friends. One of a number of his ideas was to mount a conservation parade on behalf of the tropical forest, but his friends suggested he had been too long in the United States. A parade wouldn't work, they said. Sri Lankans were not exhibitionists.

Despite the skepticism, Rudran explored the idea of a parade, talking to schools along a ten-mile stretch of road that led from the suburbs into the major city of that region. He explained the danger of losing the remaining lowland tropical forests and handed out poster board, crayons, and paints to the children. He persuaded artist friends to produce designs for yet other posters and petitioned local businessmen for support. A soda pop manufacturer, for example, whose symbol was an elephant, donated the equivalent of $500 to print an elephant poster.

Rudran had planned that the children in each school would march a little way along the route, to be replaced by children from the next school, and so on. But once the parade began, no one dropped out. By the time they reached the city, the children from all the schools along the route and hundreds of others were surging along, a blizzard of posters held high, "stopping a lot of traffic."

There were speeches and one school group performed a specially created ballet that told a story of how the beautiful birds of the forest had to leave when it was cut down, but returned when it was reforested. The parade made headlines in all the papers and was seen on national television.

The parade is now an annual event, part of a multipronged grassroots public education program in wildlife and habitat conservation. Rudran confesses that public education is quite a difficult task, but it did help get Sri Lankan administrators to establish four new national parks.

Lunch at an end at Front Royal, the Indian journalist joins two colleagues from the People's Republic of China in collating and analyzing the data from their project of the last weeks, a study they call "Time Budgets of Père David's Deer."

The key to Rudran's course is on-the-job training in the kinds of techniques and skills necessary to managing wildlife. For much of the course, class is broken down into small units of two, three, or four, that do useful research: at Front Royal there are always more questions to be answered, not just about the exotic animals present but also other residents—from white-tailed deer to bluebirds. Indeed, if humankind ever truly understands the details of life among white-tailed deer, Rudran's on-the-job training course will have provided an important fraction of the total knowledge.

On one occasion, most of the members of the class were seated in a van parked along a gravel road looking down a hill to a point where, earlier, a cannon net had been hidden across a route known to be frequented by white-tailed deer. The group waited patiently, spying deer far off, watching as they would approach the net, then wander off. The point of the exercise was, at the right moment, to fire two explosive charges propelling two iron weights into the air. The weights, attached to the ends of the net would draw it, nearly instantaneously, over an unwary deer so that it could be fitted with a radio transmitter on a collar. This day the deer proved cautious, but in the meantime, one of the group spotted movement of black fur in the grass behind the van. All eyes swung rearward, as a skunk made its way toward the gravel road.

"How beautiful!" said several of the group. The skunk disappeared, emerging in the grass on the other side of the road. It had learned to use a culvert to cross the road. This became a matter of fascinated discussion, as was the skunk itself, a creature of beauty and mystery as wondrous to the group as a cheetah would be to a Canadian.

The course provides whole-group activities—lectures by visiting wildlife experts and field trips, in this case to nearby national parks to observe the interpretive programs, and to the National Zoo in Washington. But it is when the group breaks up into teams to perform specific tasks that some particularly important learning takes place.

One team, equipped with technical advice on the use of radio transmitters and antennas, might analyze the home range of local deer. Taking regularly scheduled readings of the whereabouts of bugged deer, they would enter their findings on a map, each point accompanied by the date, the time of day, and other information (some of the listening devices can tell if the deer is resting, feeding, or moving about).

In due course, one can project a series of points on the map showing a coherent pattern of where the deer go and where they don't— i.e., their home range. Then comes the tricky part. One can draw a simple ellipse around the points and say that is the home range and compute it into a numerical quantity—a certain number of acres, or hectares, or square miles. Or one can draw another kind of line around it by a technique called the harmonic means, wherein a computer uses the average distance between all neighboring points. Or

one can connect the outermost points as in follow-the-dots into a shape called the minimum convex polygon. Three different home-range sizes emerge, all based on the same data; all three are correct. What becomes clear from this to the future wildlife manager is that in comparing the home range of an animal over time, it is necessary to know which method the previous researcher was using, so that apples will be compared to apples.

One team might census all of the vegetation eaten by deer, another investigate precisely what predators—snakes, raccoons—account for how much infant mortality among bluebirds. Still others check the effects of competition with tree swallows and house sparrows for the hundreds of bluebird boxes at Front Royal. Useful field techniques learned, useful data produced. Several from Rudran's course have subsequently been billeted at United States universities and have continued research at Front Royal to obtain advanced degrees.

The program is tailored to the student's needs. One year, two Pakistani reserve managers were present: already executives of a sort, they did not need detailed experience in one or another field technique but instead desired an overview. And so Rudran assigned them the task of producing a full-blown strategy for how to lever into greater importance among the priorities of the Pakistan government the entire business of wildlife management—then a stepchild caught between the Pakistan ministries of forestry and agriculture. For the gentle revolutionary from Sri Lanka, there is no natural break in the continuum of wildlife education—it is as important to collar a minister as it is to collar an ungulate.

The program is unique, itself a marvel of bureaucratic cooperation, being funded and actively assisted not only by the Smithsonian and the World Wildlife Fund-U.S., but by the U.S. Fish and Wildlife Service, the Agency for International Development, the New York Zoological Society, and many other agencies. During the rest of the year, after the summer sessions in Front Royal, Rudran makes house calls, traveling throughout the Third World to find new recruits, but chiefly to give his course on the road. He has trained future wildlife managers in dozens of nations. (Not surprisingly, he put in a stint at Poço das Antas Biological Reserve in Brazil, training local zoology students in the management of the golden lion tamarins.)

On the day Rudran had pressed his radical schemes on the young Indian journalist, he expressed a wish for more funds and time to publish a newsletter so that his far-flung alumni could establish an influential network of wildlife managers. "It can be lonely off in the bush." A title for the newsletter sprang to mind: Rudran's Sixth Column. He also wished that his course were not so unique, or that there were more such avenues for trained people to resolve conservation problems.

Shortly afterward, the Indian journalist and his Chinese colleagues explained their project with the Père David's deer. They had engaged in three days of observation of the herd—twelve hours per day. They had been especially interested in the pecking order, if any, among the harem of females. They had noticed that females would quite frequently march up to others lying placidly on the ground and

Summer at the center finds students from Asia, Africa, and Latin America undergoing intensive hands-on training in wildlife management. They practice techniques as simple as direct observation and as complex as radio tracking, all under the tutelage of Rudy Rudran (shown above on the right).

(Previous pages) A female sable antelope (left). A newborn sable, one of many born at the center, tries to suckle (right).

butt them. Those butted would get up and give their places to the aggressors.

In advance, the team determined thirteen different kinds of behavior to be noted, each behavior having several subcategories. The entire list of behaviors, each given a shorthand label, amounted to thirty-four. All were to be noted based on three different methods of observation. The first is called a scan. Every half-hour the entire herd is observed, animal by animal, and each animal's location, behavior of the moment, nearest neighbor recorded. This takes about ten minutes.

Then there is a "focal animal" observation, where everything a given animal does for five minutes is carefully noted. And third there is the "opportunistic" sample: if a female suddenly decides to butt another, for example, the ensuing behavior is recorded. (These methods of observation were precisely those employed by Inês Castro to follow the progress of the untrained group of golden lion tamarins.)

Holding up a handful of exquisitely neat charts that he and his Chinese colleagues had drawn, the Indian journalist said: "You see? We put all the events—who does what to whom—in a matrix like this. You can see the behaviors in a linear way. The pecking order just pops right out at you."

"What's important," he went on, "is that we have learned the real techniques for doing this kind of study. Now we don't make subjective judgments about these things. We can let the data do the interpreting." He grinned.

"I guess Dr. Rudy has given me a lot to think about, hasn't he?" asked the young Indian rhetorically, and he was clearly not thinking about matrices of behavioral data but about some of his heroes, about human nature and quiet revolutions, and about the coupling of science—the use of meticulously obtained data—with an effective passion for wildlife.

GENE KEEPERS

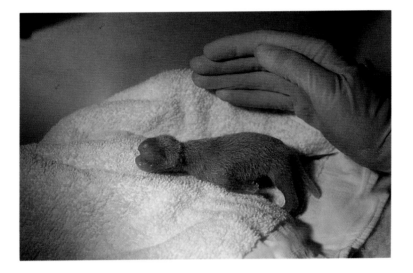

The doe hesitated, exquisitely delicate, backlit in the frame of a barn door. A rough-hewn man named Tim Portillo called her name, and she stepped deftly through the doorway, clearly defying gravity so light was the touch of her hooves on the dirt floor as she approached the man. He patted her on the head. She was an Eld's deer, about three feet high at the shoulder, and Portillo had high hopes for her.

For the time being she and a handful of her kind were temporary residents of the recently built Rivinus Barn located on an upland portion of the Conservation and Research Center. Portillo was at the time an assistant to Christen Wemmer in reproductive biological technology.

The rest of the Eld's deer at the center were not far away, in three enclosures built on a south-facing slope where the sun produces the most warmth year-round. Eld's deer are native to Southeast Asia. In their warm natural homeland, they are not doing well at all. They are timid creatures, befitting their fragility, and their hillside here in Virginia is covered with brush. One can stand for a long time on the hill facing their enclosures before seeing one of them reach its head up to browse on a low branch. When they bear young, it is a special challenge for the keepers. Eld's deer are hard to spot in any case, preferring life in the undergrowth, so it is difficult to tell when a female is pregnant. Finding the young is even more arduous. To do so, the keepers have to walk every foot of the enclosure—part of the constant trade-off between a desirable privacy and a necessary paternalism.

The nearly tame resident of Rivinus Barn submitted even to the touch of a stranger, a moist, black nose twitching, dark, wet eyes bespeaking a controlled sense of caution.

"These deer were hand-raised," explained Portillo. "They were halter-trained. We want them as tame as possible because we have to work very closely with them. That one over there has a jogger's pedometer on its neck collar so we can keep track of its movement." Indeed, Portillo planned to play a trick on this deer, fooling Mother Nature—or at least that portion of Mother Nature that resides in the cells of the deer.

There are many ways to think about the nature of life and one relatively new concept that has arisen among biologists (but is not shared by all of them) is the notion of the selfish gene. Stated simply, it recognizes that virtually everything needed to create a living adult creature (aside from the right environment) is present at birth, encoded in the genes—specifically in a long helical strand of amino acids called DNA—and any creature with largely the same DNA as another will turn out to be the same species. This is not new. The original insight is that any given member of a species, any living animal, is in fact subordinate to the survival of its particular brand of DNA. In this way of thinking, all of the physique, the behavior, the experience of an individual is merely temporary window dressing for the perpetuation of the species' DNA: the cells and bodies of individual animals are simply momentary soldiers marching to the incessant drumbeat of molecular determination. With the matter put thus, or even in a less reductionist manner, there arises a certain compelling logic for those who would manage wildlife in captivity or in the wild.

The management of animal populations now requires the management of genes. Preserving the genetic composition that made the species a success in the wild, or at least decelerating the less fortunate adaptations that can occur in captivity, is a modern necessity. It is simply not enough, as has been the case in the past, to try to provide zoo animals with a healthy and long life, as worthy as that goal may be. A long life for an individual does not, by the inescapable logic of the new zoo, ensure the survival of a species, and in some cases in this very real world it may even be counterproductive. Zoo managers must worry about inbreeding these days. Any creature that arises from the mating of parents necessarily inherits from two different sets of genes. Each gene is essentially a message that carries instructions for one aspect of the developing organism. In the case of tallness, for example, each parent has a segment on the DNA chain that speaks of height, and the height instructions of both parents are combined in the offspring's own genes. The founder of genetics, a monk named Gregor Mendel, found that if one crossed two tall plants of the same species, one got mostly tall plants. In such offspring the height gene, as it were, could be expressed as *TT*, a gene that called for tallness from both parents. Similarly, two short plants would probably produce a *tt* gene, calling for a short offspring. Cross a short and a tall plant and one usually gets a gene that says *Tt* and a tall plant because the gene for tallness dominates the gene for shortness, which is recessive.

(Previous page, left) A shy Eld's deer is briefly visible among the tall grass before fleeing to the thick cover it prefers to hide in.

(Previous page, right) Despite the intensive care this newborn giant panda was given, the tiny animal succumbed to infection a few days after its birth.

(Right) At the National Zoo's Conservation and Research Center, keepers raise some of the Eld's deer born there. These hand-reared animals can be more easily managed for studies of their behavior and reproductive biology.

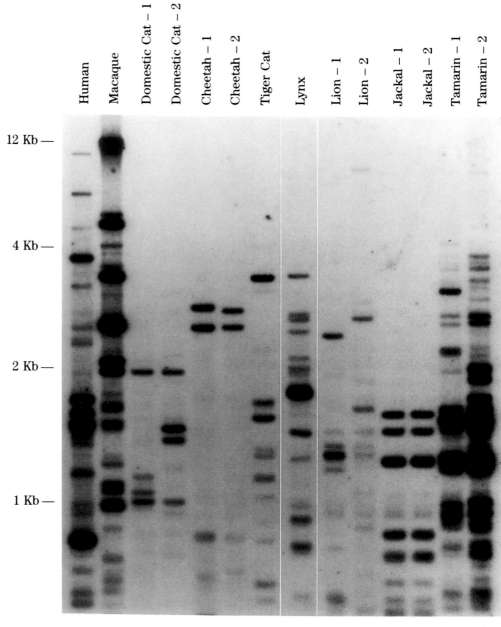

*Hae*III
Probe: 33.15

It is not at all so simple, of course. There is plenty of room for diversity. Mutations of genes, sometimes deriving from the activity of natural radioactivity playing on the delicate structure of molecules, can be passed along to the next generation. They are like typos in a series of general messages, and they are usually deleterious. Because of the random appearance of such typos and the remarkable amount of mixing of genes that goes on in the course of generations of breeding, virtually every organism has some recessive genes lurking in its DNA masked by dominant genes. But traits dictated by recessive genes (most often harmful) will frequently come to the fore if both parents have some recessive genes for the same characteristic.

Livestock and plant breeders and, perhaps most visibly, dog breeders worked with these probabilities for centuries before they were fully understood to produce special strains of creatures suited to particular purposes—a deliberate tinkering with genes. Carried too far, such experimentation can unleash a host of recessive genes, some of which lead not just to a pointier nose for Lassie, but to congenital hip dysplasia for German shepherds. So it is with zoo animals. Small populations, as in zoos, are likely to be inbred if their breeding is unmanaged. Two parents, or founders, can flood the population with their genes, and eventually the harmful recessive genes they harbored become manifest. In extreme cases, this is called an inbreeding depression. But most people in zoos did not recognize this as a special problem until three researchers at the National Zoo published some surprizing findings in 1979.

Before then, most zoos typically managed their own small collections of many different species, and thus inbreeding within species became fairly common. Typically, such inbreeding did not result so much in freakish congenital effects, but in reduced viability of young and also in reduced fecundity when breeding did occur. While this problem was generally well known among breeders of livestock and of special strains of laboratory animals, and since it was clear that some species actually do inbreed frequently without noticeably harmful effects, it was not clear that inbreeding was necessarily bad for zoo populations. Part of the uncertainty lay in the fact that zoo records were sparse and scattered and individual animals were not always identified; also one could look at such longtime captive populations as Père David's deer and see little problem despite a lengthy history of inbreeding. Furthermore, few zoos had the financial resources to perform sophisticated research, and beyond that most zoo scientists tended to be generalists, not specialists in such esoteric fields as population genetics.

In the late 1970s, Katherine Ralls, of the National Zoo's research staff, and Kristin Brugger and Jonathan Ballou, who were supported by FONZ, undertook an analysis of sixteen species of captive ungulates, correlating juvenile mortality positively to levels of inbreeding. The study included various deer and antelope species along with Indian elephants, zebras, giraffes, and pygmy hippopotamuses. The facts were, as they often are, implacable. In fifteen species, juvenile mortality was higher among inbred offspring than among offspring of unrelated parents. Detailed analysis allowed the researchers to rule out other factors such as birth season, birth order, and even management improvements over the course of the study. In one species, Dorcas gazelles, most offspring of unrelated parents survived even the traumas of being captured and transported, while inbred offspring frequently died of either starvation or medical problems and infections not found among the other calves.

These results were a bombshell. Zoos had to recognize that previous practices were not in the best interest of their animals: a new course was imperative. The news was disconcerting for wildlife conservationists since many large endangered mammals, from ungulates to primates like the gorilla, now existed in relatively small populations

(Left) With a technique called gel electrophoresis, which produces a "picture" of proteins encoded in DNA, scientists can assess the degree of genetic similarity between different species and between individuals of the same species. Increasingly, the tools of molecular biology are being used by zoo biologists to assess the genetic diversity of small populations of endangered species.

(Below and following page) Dorcas gazelles and zebras were among the many species of ungulates studied by National Zoo scientists to demonstrate that inbreeding in small populations increases infant mortality and must therefore be prevented by zoo managers.

in their ever-decreasing natural habitats. No doubt the same inbreeding was taking place in the wild among populations that had normally "outbred" naturally. A new course was called for in this realm as well. The implications of the zoo's study were heeded widely and soon incorporated into strategies for maintaining healthy populations of endangered species.

The studies of Ralls and her colleagues continued, covering forty-four mammal species altogether, including a variety of non-ungulate species, and in 1983 it was announced that in ninety-three percent of the species studied, mortality in inbred offspring was higher than in the young of outbreeding parents. Such findings stamped out for good most recessive tendencies among zoos to ignore inbreeding. However, other genetic problems were recognized in small captive populations, one being a number of instances of congenital defects such as cataracts, skeletal defects, and diaphragmatic hernias (as in the golden lion tamarins). Because of the small size of the samples in most zoo populations, it was difficult to determine exactly how these defects were inherited, if indeed they were genetic. Just how and whether to try to rid captive populations of such defects remained to be seen, but by 1986 interzoo cooperation in the management of captive animals as single populations was the increasingly common modus operandi here and abroad.

Indeed, cooperation and coordination became the keystone for the then-emerging plans for sustained captive breeding of captive animals, a task clearly to be accomplished without the regular infusions of new blood from the wild that were previously taken for granted. New technologies and careful attention to the mathematical business of population genetics were crucial to the effort. Precision studies of rapidly breeding species such as fruit flies where several carefully monitored generations could be produced in days or weeks and analyzed by computer supplied the basic knowledge that would be applied to populations where life spans are long and generations can take on human (or greater) dimensions. Zoos were confronted with the need to think in centuries. As the time dimension expanded, other considerations contracted. Endangered populations could be as small as, in the case of Speke's gazelle, four individuals. Thus, population managers had to experiment with miniaturization, the creation of stable heritages from small arrays of genes. Moreover, it is just in such small arrays that things can go awry almost overnight.

Some genetic changes aptly suit individuals for their environment or for a sudden change in environment. Others may render individuals unfit in one way or another. A species is thus something like extemporaneous music, ongoing variations on a theme, some of which work and some of which don't. The sense of the music remains, however, always kept interesting (viable) by subtle changes. Each gene can be thought of as a musical chord made of several notes of which some dominate.

Inbreeding tends to reduce the chord to one note in this analogy. The smaller the breeding population the fewer notes from which to make up chords: eventually a chord with a single note is reached. This tendency is active in small, natural, outbreeding populations as well;

it is called genetic drift.

The range of genes—the richness of the chords—tends to increase naturally by the random process of genetic mutation. But at the same time it declines as individuals bearing rare genes either die before they reproduce or otherwise fail to sound their particular notes in the population. In small populations, as in most zoo situations, the rate of loss of genes by this drift is likely to exceed the rate of production of new ones by random mutation, so there is a built-in bias in zoo populations toward the one-note form of genetic music.

Like music, genetics is a mathematical affair involving a limited though complicated range of choices and combinations. In the early eighties zoos came to realize that they needed to manipulate the harmonics of genes. The world of the zoo had become at once more complex in the skills demanded of it and more simplified in its purpose.

Toward this end, the American Association of Zoological Parks and Aquariums adopted an innovative program called the Species Survival Plan and initially focused on a few species especially in need of intensive captive breeding efforts. By 1989 there were fifty species in the program, of which the National Zoo was actively engaged with over a dozen, including the golden lion tamarin, the red panda, and the maned wolf. The criteria for selection are chiefly that the species is imperiled in the wild or is the single representative of a genus or family. There are other practical considerations as well: there must be a high probability of successful captive breeding; there must be an organized and willing group of professionals with the necessary support; and there must be information.

Traditionally zoos have not been the most precise record keepers and, obviously, to manage a captive population along sound genetic lines, genealogies are of the essence. Katherine Ralls has said, in fact, that it was probably only at the National Zoo that she could have performed her ground-breaking analysis of the effects of inbreeding, since so few other zoos had such complete and accurate records of births, deaths, and individual identities.

A considerable impetus for record keeping in the zoo world came from an unlikely, outside source, an army man named Marvin Jones. Jones was keen on zoos and traveled widely with the army. He made zoo genealogies a hobby. It was he who, in the late sixties, began the golden lion tamarin studbook. After retirement he went to work at the San Diego Zoo. There his work inspired a program begun by yet another outsider, a biochemist named Ulysses S. Seal who worked at a veteran's hospital and began the International Species Inventory System (ISIS) in 1975. Now located at the Minneapolis Zoo, ISIS houses inside a computer as much genealogical data as can be obtained on zoo and laboratory animals. All in all, eighty percent of U.S. zoos report birth and death information to ISIS (an acronym which harks back to the ancient Egyptian goddess of fertility). It is with such records that a Species Survival Plan can be developed.

Once a species is selected for this high-priority treatment, representatives from the zoos that house the species meet and appoint one of themselves to be overall manager of that species and one to be keeper of the species studbook. Then a specific plan must be developed. The goals in each case are usually similiar: establish as diverse a founding group as possible, preferably with ten to twenty founders; increase the species population rapidly to zoo carrying capacity and then spread it around among zoos; equalize the genetic contributions of each founder; and monitor the population to avoid inbreeding problems. Each species requires different strategies depending on such factors as the number and age of the founders, the degree of their relatedness, the overall population size, and the availability of the animal in the wild.

Another important factor is precisely what end result is desired. Is this an animal to be bred in captivity so that it can eventually be returned to the wild? Or is it a newly collected animal to be adapted to captivity for long-term maintenance in zoos, or one that lives and will forever live in zoos, being extinct elsewhere, its habitat gone?

With the golden lion tamarins, the plan called for breeding the population rapidly to carrying capacity, and then slowing down the rate of reproduction and maximizing outbreeding so that the genetic diversity achieved would be retained longer. With the Speke's gazelle in the Saint Louis Zoo, the goal of avoiding inbreeding had to go by the boards: the strategy was in fact reversed. Here the North American population of fifteen animals was founded by one male and three females and had become severely inbred; the likelihood of obtaining more from the wild was near zero, given the chronic war in its native habitat in Ethiopia and Somalia. The plan recommended that inbred parents be used as much as possible to produce inbred young even when some outbreeding would be possible. The intent of this kind of blitz on the gazelle's gene is to select for those genes that have enabled the animals to tolerate inbreeding and to eliminate (via mortality) the deleterious recessive genes that cause inbreeding depression. The expectation was that even a normally outbreeding population can adapt to mild inbreeding. The early results were encouraging: the population soon doubled and gazelles born from planned matings had higher survival rates than those from earlier, unplanned matings. But this kind of manipulation, while saving the gazelle, produces inevitable and profound genetic changes. It is highly doubtful that any Speke's gazelles from North American zoos could ever survive in the wild. They are truly different animals.

Many theoretical and practical questions still needed answering, so in the summer of 1984, Katherine Ralls and Jonathan Ballou organized a week-long workshop on genetic management at the Conservation and Research Center attended by thirty population geneticists and prominent zoo biologists. One question addressed was how big a captive population should be to maintain maximum genetic diversity over time. It depends, it was decided, to a great degree on the generation time of the species. If one wanted to maintain ninety percent of the animals' genetic diversity during a breeding program that was to extend over two hundred years, one would need one thousand mice (whose generation time is one year) and only forty elephants (generation time, about twenty-five years). Another question addressed was the matter of selection in captivity. Animal species adapt over time to

Recent molecular biology analyses show that the Sumatran and Bornean subspecies of orangutans—once allowed to interbreed in zoos—are as different genetically as common and pygmy chimpanzees, which are considered distinct species. As a result, zoos now manage the two orang subspecies to prevent further hybridization.

changing environments and in a long-term captive breeding program zoo animals will of necessity adapt to their artificial environment, leading to changes in food preferences or reproductive schedules or reproductive rates. Such changes often make the animals easier to maintain in captivity, but could also render them unfit for the wild.

Population geneticists here and abroad are developing computerized means of examining past pedigrees of captive animals and projecting future pedigrees to determine not only what genes of given founders will eventually drop out of the population but how soon. These programs are becoming critical to the development of Species Survival Plans.

From matters large (populations), discussion at the workshop moved to matters small (molecules). The National Zoo, working with Stephen O'Brien at the National Cancer Institute in Fort Dietrich, Maryland, has been using various techniques for analyzing genetic diversity at the molecular level, the chief of these being protein electrophoresis. This technique provides measurements of variation among certain structural proteins of the genes and can answer both theoretical and practical questions. Through this method it was determined that giant pandas are more closely related evolutionarily to bears, while red pandas are related to raccoons. A researcher at the zoo used the technique to discover that the severely threatened wild golden lion tamarins were more inbred than the captive population. In planning breeding programs for captive populations it is used to judge whether the members of a species are genetically like enough to sustain some inbreeding. Also at the workshop there was discussion of how accurate this micro-technique might be—perhaps crucial genetic messages do not occur at the structural points that protein electrophoresis examines—but such criticisms were not nitpicking: they represent fine-tuning, or what is called care.

Much of the meeting at the center was what Ballou indeed called "fine-tuning," but there was general agreement about the theory by which genetic diversity can be maintained. "Nothing about the theory," said Ralls, "suggests that it can't be done."

Of course there are practical obstacles to overcome. Proper genetic management takes time, energy, and money spent in collecting and analyzing data. Producing and maintaining an international studbook for a species is a herculean task, and for many species deserving of such management, present records of breeding histories are simply inadequate or nonexistent. There are also the intractable constraints of space. The average size of zoos in the United States is fifty-five acres: combined, they occupy a mere twenty-two thousand acres. All the zoos in the world could fit into the borough of Brooklyn.

Obviously, even in the best of circumstances, some godlike choices have to be made. Not all zoos have the resources—either financial or human—to participate in Species Survivial Plans. Furthermore, a handful of zoo managers are not yet convinced of the danger of inbreeding; some are reluctant to incur the expense of importing a breeding male from another zoo when a population geneticist informs them that the breeding male they already have is becoming too dominant in the gene pool.

The zoo exhibits "surplus" ruffed lemurs—animals whose genes are already well represented in the zoo population of this endangered species and are thus not part of the breeding program.

Another practical problem inherent in genetic management—and one also related to space—is success. The price of success can be too many animals for the space available. In the first place, zoo animals tend to live longer than their wild counterparts, thanks to excellent food and medical care plus freedom from predators. Then as breeding conditions are improved and infant survival rates climb with a reduction in inbreeding, overpopulation is virtually inevitable. It may soon be a problem with the golden lion tamarins as it was with the National Zoo's Barbary macaques. Beginning in 1950 with four animals, the macaque population rose to thirty-one by 1970. In fact the zoo has been able to supply all U.S. zoos that now have macaques with breeding stock as a result of its population boom; the zoos now have to go to Europe and Africa for unrelated stock. Meanwhile fashions changed and interest in these macaques declined. What is a zoo to do with "surplus" animals, if other zoos either aren't interested in providing them with a home or already have a sufficient number? There are minimum population sizes based on long-term genetic considerations and maximum sizes based on available space, while the fine calculations concern how much space to devote to one species when space is a prime consideration. Populations thus have to be controlled by one or more of several approaches. The first is to regulate reproductive rates either by keeping males and females separate or by implanting birth control devices in the females. This latter was implemented with the Barbary macaques at the National Zoo, but as Ballou says, "Often it's very, very tricky to manipulate reproductive rates," and doing so can, in some cases, bias the population in favor of older animals or those whose genes are already well represented.

Another alternative is to control survivorship—in a word, euthanasia. This is hard for anyone to swallow, especially keepers and curators. The public does not usually understand that to save endangered animals in captivity it is essential to think in terms of the species, of populations, rather than individual animals. People are most upset by the idea of euthanizing "charismatic megafauna," big, popular animals such as tigers and gorillas, who often even have names. Such was the case with Siberian tigers that, by 1984, had reached the carrying capacity of U.S. zoos for the species—about 250. Earlier these animals had been bred widely in captivity: reproduction was then drastically curtailed. The result was a population in which a few of ten founders had provided a disproportionate amount of genes and one in which too great a proportion of animals were past reproduction age.

Strategy from the American Association of Zoological Parks and Aquariums called for the breeding of younger animals in the population to stabilize the tigers' genetics and demography, meaning that some older animals would have to make way. When the situation arose in 1982 at the Detroit Zoo, a public outcry led to an injunction against euthanizing an old male. Unless people understand and accept the goal of a healthy species—which requires that the species be invested with rights that take precedence over those of the individual—no Species Survival Plan will work in the long run.

Zoo officials are keenly aware of this ethical dilemma, of the need for the utmost care in directing the lives of their wards, and of the

Rare red pandas are part of the Species Survival Plan, which ensures that all North American zoos cooperate to manage the red pandas in their collections as a single breeding population.

A population explosion among Barbary macaques led the zoo to limit further reproduction by implanting female macaques with a hormonal contraceptive.

need for public education. In 1984 the National Zoo, recognizing the intellectual, emotional, ethical, and public relations problems that arise from the logic of genetic management, formed an Animal Welfare Committee. The committee regularly meets to discuss such knotty questions as keeping animals that are not part of the breeding program and handling surplus animals. It also regularly inspects the zoo's facilities to be sure that animals on and off exhibition have enough space and comfortable living conditions. The committee has developed its own education program for all hands at the zoo, and FONZ regularly keeps its members abreast of developments in the science and technology of captive breeding.

Nevertheless, it is difficult to persuade the press and the public that killing off a healthy member of an endangered species humanely can be a positive contribution (however discomfiting) to saving the species. It will take a greater public awareness of the complexity of the population manager's task and perhaps some reflection before this principle is understood. In the world of animal management, the only catastrophe worse than the loss of an animal is the loss of a species: once a species is gone, it is gone forever.

A third solution is to manipulate the other variable: space. Some zoos are actively seeking to buy up extra land outside cities and some private wild animal parks are assisting them, but until an aware citizenry allocates the funds necessary for such expansion, draconian choices will simply have to be made more and more frequently.

The American public and press appreciate success, the more spectacular the better. Quiet triumphs like the breeding of the obscure tiger cats at the Front Royal Center rarely make headlines, but new breeding technologies unfailingly captivate the public imagination.

In May 1984 a quarter horse in the Louisville Zoo made headlines by giving birth to a zebra. A couple of weeks later, an eland, a relatively

135

common antelope, gave birth to a much rarer bongo baby in the Cincinnati Zoo. And there was news from London that a donkey there would soon give birth to a zebra. These were results of interspecies embryo transfer. Even earlier, at the Bronx Zoo, a gaur had been born from a Holstein cow. Neither artificial insemination nor embryo transfer were altogether new. Both had been practiced with great success over the years among cattle, horses, and humans; indeed the dairy industry had been transferring embryos since the 1950s. But the bongo born in the Cincinnati Zoo was a first of several kinds.

The Bronx Zoo's gaur had been implanted surgically in the Holstein cow. In the case of the surrogate eland mother, there had been no surgery. Also, the bongo birth was the first case of transcontinental embryo transfer: the animal had been conceived nine months earlier in the Los Angeles Zoo. The embryos—about one hundred of them— had then been extracted from the bongo mother and flown in vials to Ohio, where the healthiest ones were implanted in the eland.

There were other firsts in the offing. In October 1984 a female eland was born to an eland mother twenty-seven months after conception rather than the usual nine months. The embryo calf had been extracted from its mother seven days after conception and frozen in liquid nitrogen at −196 degrees C for eighteen months and then implanted. Thus this calf was the first frozen embryo of an exotic and the first to be implanted. These world records are muddled a bit by the fact that the London Zoo, during the Cincinnati mother eland's nine months of pregnancy, had themselves frozen marmoset embryos, implanted them, and seen them born—all before the eland calf emerged. The urge to be first struck some as unseemly in this era of zoo cooperation. Nevertheless, there was little doubt these artificial technologies offered renewed hope that at least some endangered species could be given a second chance. Their potential was included in the strategies of the Species Survival Plan, for they coincide with the goals of increasing fertility and genetic diversity. They also promise a convenient solution to a considerable difficulty in arranging marriages among captive populations: it is dangerous to tranfer large animals across the country or intercontinentally (a bongo, for example, is valued at about $25,000, and to lose one to the exigencies of travel would be two kinds of tragedy).

Artificial insemination involves first the collection of semen from the male. In some animals this can be done by arranging for the male to copulate with a dummy female. There is such a leather and wood dummy at Front Royal: it looks like a cross between an oversized rocking horse and a gymnastic device. Most species won't be fooled by such impostors, but their semen can be collected by administering an electric current when the animal has been anesthetized. Indeed, with the exception of rhinoceros and a few other species, it will soon be standard practice to make such a collection when a male is, for whatever other necessity, anesthetized. The semen can then be used immediately or frozen and stored to be implanted later in a ready female.

Yet artificial insemination is tricky and has been used successfully in only about a half-dozen exotic species, including certain primates,

With zoo populations as large as 250 to 500 individuals necessary to ensure the long-term genetic health of many species, spacious breeding centers such as the National Zoo's Conservation and Research Center become increasingly important to saving endangered species.

carnivores, ungulates, and birds. Wild species are just that—wild, and often obstinate. Handling them can be dangerous, so the risks from any sort of manipulation must always be weighed. Also, repeated intervention with an animal may produce just the sort of stress that will interfere with the reproductive process itself. The semen, once collected, must be stored in a culture medium at about 30 degrees C if it is to be used within a few hours, or frozen if the interval is to be greater. From species to species, the semen's ability to maintain fertility during storage may vary widely. Furthermore, the female reproductive cycle must be well understood in order to time insemination effectively, a real challenge in little-studied rare exotics.

The difference between domestic and exotic artificial insemination is fundamental. In domestics, it is used not to aid fertility and not to increase genetic diversity, but to perpetuate a desirable trait among an already fertile population. A prize bull may properly flood the world with thousands of offspring. On the other hand, an unrelated pair of gorillas in the Melbourne Zoo had been reared together and, hence, avoided each other sexually as if they were brother and sister. Here artificial insemination was used to bridge a behavioral obstacle to mating. Chia-Chia, the giant panda of the London Zoo, successfully fathered a cub in Spain via artificial insemination, thus avoiding the arduous trip himself. He was also used as an emergency auxiliary for Hsing-Hsing, who in 1984 had mated unsuccessfully, officials thought, with Ling-Ling. (After the cub's birth and subsequent death, it was determined by blood analysis to be Hsing-Hsing's.)

Transferring embryos—especially from one species to another—involves all the caveats that apply to artificial insemination. It requires delicate interference in several reproductive cycles, plus an understanding of the immune systems of the creatures involved—that is, which species will tolerate the embryo of another and produce the placenta necessary for its development. It is little wonder that embryo transfers have so far been achieved only with exotic animals that are related to domestic animals.

The technique, in brief, begins with insemination (usually artificial) of a female who has previously been given hormones to impel her to superovulate. Here again, which hormone for which species must be worked out in detail. After a few days (again, how many for each species?), the embryos must be found, flushed out, inspected for viability, and preserved, either briefly or indefinitely by freezing. The hormonal balance of the surrogate mother must also be adjusted in order to prepare her system for the introduced embryos.

The development of reliable breeding techniques occupies the people at the National Zoo. They prefer progress to headlines. Scientists generally seek to study replicable events to adequately test their ideas. So far, there have been few repetitions in the business of embryo transfers and little of detail published in the scientific literature: the field itself is, of course, embryonic. While some people are inclined to call it flashy high-tech activity, most admit it does raise a great number of important theoretical and practical scientific questions about exotic species—chiefly about reproductive biology—and to the extent that it helps answer these questions, it will have served a

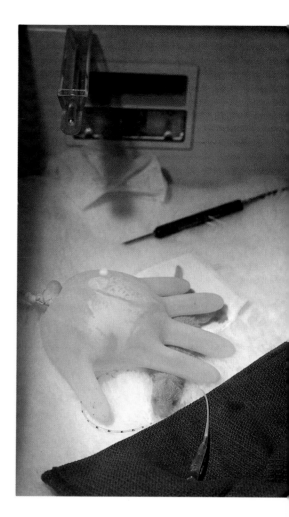

Sometimes homey improvisation replaces high technology in zoo biology: A surgical glove filled with warm water comforts a sick newborn giant panda.

purpose. Few zoo managers think that artificial breeding is to be preferred over the more natural modes. Ultimately, however, artificial breeding could provide the fallback position for a species facing extinction: a species could be maintained perhaps indefinitely in a freezer until the time was propitious for its reemergence.

In the spirit of scientific investigation, the Eld's deer in Rivinus Barn was in 1984 unwittingly being groomed as a producer of eggs that would then be implanted in white-tailed deer as surrogate mothers. The scimitar-horned oryxes were being eyed with similar intent. But by 1986 zoo scientists had withdrawn the Eld's deer from the plan to experiment with embryo transfer. As Christen Wemmer explained: "We decided that we had such a good-sized study group of Eld's deer that we'd be better off doing other kinds of physiological-behavioral monitoring of their reproduction. The animals are delicate and the transfer technique is intrusive. We decided we could get more scientific knowledge by less intervention." But plans for embryo transplants in the hardier oryx were still being considered.

Meanwhile, studies of reproductive biology led to the solidification of a concerted research program in the National Zoo's Department of Animal Health. Orchestrated by David Wildt, a research physiologist with that department and carried out in close association with veterinarian Mitchell Bush, the program set forth to increase basic knowledge of the reproductive strategies of little-studied species, to examine the infertility problems of animals with reproductive difficulties, and, with such information, to propagate certain species by artificial techniques.

In the early 1980s, Stephen O'Brien, of the National Cancer Institute, Bush, and Wildt made an extraordinary and shocking discovery through joint research. It was known that cheetahs in captivity were extremely difficult to breed. Many great kings had throughout history kept thousands of captive cheetahs. The sixteenth-century Mongol emperor, Akbar the Great, had strenuously sought to breed his nearly one thousand cheetahs, allowing them to run free in the palace, but only a single litter was ever produced. That litter was the last born in captivity until a pair of cheetahs at the Philadelphia Zoo produced a litter in 1956. Since then, only ten to fifteen percent of wild-caught cheetahs have bred in captivity; the conception rate is low compared to other species; and juvenile mortality has been about thirty percent. The South African Zoo was experiencing similar difficulties and suggested that the National Zoo cooperate with them in exploring the problem, which was not restricted to captive cheetahs. It had been estimated that in wild populations (some twenty thousand animals in isolated pockets of Africa) infant mortality was about seventy percent, too high to be accounted for by predation on the infants by other carnivores, which is common.

O'Brien, Bush, and Wildt traveled to the South African Zoo's DeWildt Cheetah Research Center and obtained semen samples from eighteen male cheetahs. Upon analysis, they found that the semen contained only one-tenth the amount of spermatazoa usually found in domestic cats and that more than seventy percent of the cells were

structurally abnormal. Something clearly was up.

The researchers went on to draw blood samples from fifty of the DeWildt cheetahs, male and female, and from six captive cheetahs. They submitted the blood to a series of elaborate tests in laboratories back home, isolating and examining fifty-two different proteins from each sample. There was no variation whatsoever, indicating a genetic monomorphism reminiscent of inbred mouse strains. Individuals could not be distinguished based on enzyme structural genes, proteins were far less variable than in other species, and a crucial gene complex that is actually the most variable in mammals was found to be monolithic in cheetahs. This gene complex is called the major histocompatibility complex (MHC). Responsible for much of the action of the animal's immune system, it not only serves to repel disease organisms but also to reject tissue and organ transplants.

To check on this startling find, the researchers exchanged reciprocal skin grafts between fourteen cheetahs. Normally it takes animals, including humans, about twelve days to reject a foreign graft. All of the foreign skin grafts on the cheetahs outlasted that time, many remaining healthy for more than ten weeks. The cheetahs in the wild, it seemed, were genetically nearly identical, rendering them, with their similar immune systems, extremely vulnerable to disease. Indeed, in 1982, a large number of captive cheetahs here and abroad fell to a viral epidemic, the most extreme response to viral infection reported for any feline species.

What was evident was that cheetahs had somehow encountered a genetic bottleneck in the wild. They are not predisposed to incestuous matings, according to field studies. One theory proposes that the species has evolved to an adaptive optimum and has shed its genetic variation naturally. This theory is not borne out by the facts: cheetahs really aren't that well adapted to their environment. Among other things, such as high infant mortality, a cheetah always loses in a showdown with other predators over a kill. The researchers concluded that once, or several times, in the fairly distant past, the forerunner of today's cheetah population dropped to a few individuals, perhaps because of climatic catastrophe, viral infection, or some other crisis. In any case, the cheetah, they say, "probably escaped extinction by a whisker."

The researchers subsequently returned to Africa to sample East African cheetahs living on the Serengeti Plain. The results were largely the same: genetic diversity remained low and reproductive characteristics were generally poor. These startling findings are not necessarily a death sentence for the cheetah. The researchers point out that elephant seals were hunted to the point where at the turn of the century only twenty founders were left. Under protection, the seal population has grown and thrived. As previously noted, the Speke's gazelle population, while extremely inbred, is surviving via a fairly radical genetic management scheme. The cheetah bottleneck might have occurred as long ago as the late Pleistocene (about ten thousand years ago) during a massive mammal extinction that wiped out seventy-five percent of then-extant mammal species, including various cheetah species, leaving only one whose range was severely restricted from a worldwide distribution to a few areas in Africa. If that is the case, the researchers say, perhaps most of the severely bad genes have by now been eliminated through natural selection.

This intensive reproductive research did not end with the cheetah. O'Brien, Bush, and Wildt have since studied the relationship between the loss of genetic diversity and fertility problems in several species, including the Asiatic lion. The last remnant population of Asiatic lions, only about 250 individuals strong, lives in the Gir Forest in India. As was expected by the researchers, the genetic profile of these lions varied as little as that of the cheetah. More important, Wildt's reproductive evaluations revealed very poor semen quality and low circulating testosterone concentrations. While Asiatic lions could no doubt benefit from an infusion of genetic material from their African counterparts, the solutions are not always simple. Wildlife purists recognize the Asiatic lion as a separate species, which should not be "contaminated" by genes from unrelated creatures.

The zoo's Reproductive Physiology Program, as it is now called, is growing rapidly and benefiting from the contributions of graduate students, postdoctoral fellows, and technicians. It focuses on artificial breeding technologies since these may well be the last hope for many declining species. One fundamental practice in artificial breeding is to conduct experiments on "model" species. Usually a domestic species is chosen as a research model, and what is learned from the model species is then transferred to work with endangered exotics. The model species protect endangered populations from unnecessary risk, as was demonstrated in the zoo's study of embryo transfer in domestic cats. The cats that were treated with hormones to increase the number of eggs released did not produce particularly high-quality embryos, and the pregnancy rate after transferring the embryos to surrogate mothers was also not high. This method of transfer, involving the surgical removal and implantation of embryos, would be impractical for endangered species since the pregnancy rate was so low and since the surgery could compromise an animal's future reproductive potential by damaging reproductive organs.

In vitro or "test-tube" fertilization is a promising technology for artificial breeding. Practiced in humans for years, it is now used in exotics both to create embryos and to study sperm-penetrating ability in species that produce high numbers of abnormal sperm. Egg maturation is another technique that Wildt and his associates are exploring—the laboratory incubation of immature eggs removed directly from the ovaries. Once the eggs have aged sufficiently, they can be mixed with sperm, the hoped-for outcome of the mixture being embryos. In the future, eggs may be rescued from terminally ill members of endangered species. The zoo is already experimenting with the maturation of eggs removed from animals that have been dead as long as twenty-four hours.

Of course, many of these techniques depend upon the freezer. Sperm and embryos, called germ plasm, have to be frozen if they are to be stored for a long time or transported a long distance. Cryobiology, the name for this science of freezing life, has made the concept of the "frozen zoo" a possibility. For decades zoo philosophers have

The startling finding that all captive cheetahs were near clones in their genetic makeup led National Zoo scientists to the African plains to study cheetahs in the wild. To their further surprise, the wild cheetahs too were genetically nearly identical. This may account for the cheetahs' low reproductive rates, high infant mortality, and poor resistance to disease, phenomena found in both wild and zoo populations.

considered the potential of storing germ plasm from rare species in large tanks of bone-chilling liquid nitrogen. For wildlife species, this could mean survival. Frozen germ plasm from rare animals that are already well represented in present-day populations could be stored and used to regenerate those genes in later populations. A sperm and embryo repository would also provide obvious insurance benefits if a small zoo population were devastated by a disease or epidemic. Finally, cryobiology offers the ultimate tool for genetic management, the possibility of infusing new genes into genetically stagnant captive populations. Sperm (and perhaps eventually embryos) could be collected from genetically vigorous, free-living populations and used to reintroduce "wild genes" into zoo populations.

The National Zoo's scientists have taken a leadership role in frozen germ plasm conservation. Further, the zoo's direct association with the Smithsonian, the world's foremost archival institution, makes it a logical choice as an international center for the long-term storage of genetic material from rare species. Perhaps one day the National Zoo will create a genetic archive to match the other Smithsonian archives of many kinds of masterpieces; in this case, however, it would be all the work of a single artist.

"We're really right at the beginning of the program," says Ballou, whose very title—population manager—speaks volumes about the new zoo. The people involved tend to be aware of the omnipotent role they have been forced to assume and they do not necessarily cherish the potential hubris involved.

Zoo people today—romantics in the engine room of evolution?— may seem a far cry from the anonymous attendants in the deer parks of the mandarins, but they share the same delight in the creations of nature. The essence of what humankind has always admired in these creations is their difference from each other and from ourselves—in a sense, genetic diversity. Thus we now practice data-based shifting of animals from place to place and outright intervention in families and even careers—as necessary stewardship to preserve the essence of Someone Else's plan.

To develop methods of artificial insemination for the critically endangered black-footed ferret, zoo reproductive biologists used common domestic ferrets to perfect their techniques. These four domestic ferret kits were the first of two hundred produced by artificial insemination. Should it prove necessary, the scientists are now ready to apply this reproductive technology to bolster the population of black-footed ferrets in captivity. No ferrets remain in the wild—the last few were captured for captive breeding in 1986—but the breeding program has been so successful that hopes run high for reintroduction to begin as early as 1991.

THE URGE TO KNOW

Benjamin Beck spends a lot of time just watching the gorillas in the Great Ape House, politely eyeing them over his shoulder. He hasn't yet put in a thousand hours of observation, though he has traveled to zoos in Buffalo, Columbus, and Chicago to watch their gorillas as well. Beck, the National Zoo's assistant director for exhibits, is an intense man with a neatly trimmed beard and bright eyes, an outspoken man as are so many people at the zoo. Though no sentimentalist, he is painfully aware that gorillas are in trouble—both in the wild and in captivity.

In the wild, gorillas are losing habitat at an alarming rate and are ruthlessly hunted by poachers. The entire wild population of all kinds of gorillas—mountain and lowland—is between twelve and forty-five thousand. (Gorillas are so retiring and their habitats so remote that a precise census has not been made.) Mountain gorillas have the smallest population among gorilla species. There are probably no more than five hundred individuals. Genetic management of captive gorillas, an urgent goal, is complicated by the fact that the importation of wild-caught animals is illegal. There are official ways for zoos and research institutions to arrange with the African nations in which gorillas are native to bring in wild-caught specimens, but there is little interest in doing so because even one importation could trigger increased demand, further threatening already vulnerable wild populations.

There are some six hundred gorillas in captivity in the world's zoos,

and they produce only about thirty-five offspring a year, which is about the same as the number that die each year. Added to this, the best breeders—wild-caught animals—are aging, thus becoming less productive. The conclusion, unless reproductive success and longevity are increased, is inescapable: some day there will be no gorillas in zoos. Not only is it conceivable that children might never be able to lay eyes on this largest primate, but also that zoos might not be able to provide a fallback position for this species until (and if) its condition in the wild improves. The situation obviously calls for research and action.

In some scientific circles, there is a great distinction made between pure and applied research, the latter often judged disdainfully by practitioners of the former. Such distinctions—and the snobbery associated with them—disappear like smoke in a windstorm when there is an urgent matter at the zoo, such as survival of a species or simply of a superpopular exhibit animal: any knowledge is applicable. The six gorillas at the National Zoo were a microcosm of the overall problem. None had reproduced since 1972 and three had never reproduced. Laparoscopic examination of the ovaries of the three females showed that it was not a physiological problem among the females: they all ovulated normally, once a month as in humans. This was confirmed by analysis of hormone concentration in the urine of two of the females, Femelle and M'Wasi, who were "potty" trained and provided a daily sample over a period of several months. Because the zoo did not have its own reproductive biology laboratory at that time, the samples were analyzed at the San Diego Zoo. As with some fifty other female gorillas so analyzed, the hormone levels were predictable and healthy.

It was, it seemed, largely a male problem. A survey by Beck in 1979 had shown that fewer than one-quarter of the captive male gorillas in North America had reproduced. Sperm samples suggested that half the males had less than one percent normal sperm; male sterility appeared to be widespread, for which there could be several causes. A change of venue involving new quarters and new females as well as a strict weight-loss diet caused one male to resume normal spermatogenesis. National Zoo veterinarian Mitchell Bush and reproductive physiologist David Wildt found discomforting results in the zoo's three males. Two—Nikumba and Tomoka—though actively sexual, were sterile, and the third, Hercules, was perfectly fertile but wouldn't mate—a behavioral problem.

A holistic look at the nature of gorillas elucidates their breeding problems in captivity. It embraces the evolutionary connection between physiology and behavior. In short, a male gorilla spends time as a loner, trying to entice females to join him, an act often requiring a titanic battle with another male. Once in control, the victorious male has his way unchallenged with females as they come into estrus. This is quite different from chimpanzees where several males in one group may be in constant competition for females—less by aggressive activity than by getting there first and most frequently. And compared to chimpanzees, the gorillas' testes are a relatively insignificant proportion of body weight—only 0.017 percent as opposed to the chimp's .27 percent. Researchers have found as well that the ejaculate of a gorilla

It is easy to imagine that the sad expression of gorillas reflects an awareness of their bleak chance for continued survival in the forests of Africa. Even the population of gorillas in zoos is threatened as their reproductive success is historically low. But new knowledge, gained both from field studies and zoo research, may soon brighten this gloomy forecast. Maintaining zoo gorillas in larger, more natural groups and ensuring that young animals have plenty of social experience are keys to improving the breeding of gorillas in zoos.

normally contains only about twenty percent viable sperm (less than fifty percent in a human is tantamount to infertility). In a sense, it can be said that given their social structure the male gorilla simply doesn't need a great deal of potency, and it is not hard to see this slim margin of safety being lost in the altered environment of captivity: male gorillas are sterility prone. They are also apparently a bit particular about their mates, as are the females.

In the wild, when gorillas reach maturity (age eight for females and eleven for males) they often leave their natal group, the males remaining solitary for a time, the females quickly joining another group. This practice serves to avoid inbreeding, but for years it also confused matters in zoos where typically pairs of young gorillas from the wild—often brother and sister—would not mate. The situation was further complicated by the fact that if a gorilla is taken from its society at too young an age, it simply doesn't learn social and parental skills. The solution is obvious: allow young ones to grow up with their families in a gorilla society in an environment that is as naturalistic as possible. At sexual maturity introduce them to strangers of the opposite sex. Unfortunately, this prescription is no guarantee.

Among humans, blind dates often fail: the two people just don't see anything in each other. It can be the same with gorillas. For example, at the National Zoo, the fertile male, Hercules, never mated; and one reason, it appears, is that the females didn't want him. Similarly, Sylvia, who is physiologically fertile, appeared to be a wallflower: the males simply weren't interested in her. But Sylvia has now mated with an experienced male at the Columbus Zoo, and Hercules has recently been sent to the Pittsburgh Zoo to be paired with a new female.

There is some urgency in sorting out these kinds of problems. Patiently watching the interactions of captive gorillas, Beck sought characteristics of gorilla behavior that would provide matchmakers with a powerful predictive tool. "The decisions about which gorillas should be partners have usually been based on wishful thinking," says Beck, "and you can waste a lot of valuable gorilla time putting incompatible partners together and hoping something will happen."

From his observations over time, Beck found two predictors that he says now seem almost "simpleminded." First, the male must be dominant ("I don't especially like this outcome," Beck says, "but the gorillas did it, not me.") When a male and female are first introduced, there is usually a certain amount of aggression. If the female submits, this bodes well: if she doesn't, the result will usually be increasingly serious fighting until the two must be separated. The pair is obviously incompatible. Serious fighting involves biting: normally even compatible gorilla pairs will rough up each other a bit, slapping, pushing, and pulling hair. If the female does less of this than the male over time, the male tempers his aggression, a behavioral compromise is reached, and mating is possible, even likely.

The second predictor is a behavior that Beck calls "rest near." A female gorilla must be able to walk up to a male (or vice versa) and sit down next to him without his attacking or leaving. Sylvia, Beck found, practically never got to rest near anyone.

How effective are these predictors? It may be a little early to say,

but Beck explains that once, at another zoo, he observed several pairs of recently introduced gorillas for a while and on a Friday said that only one pair would be compatible, based on the dominant behavior of the male and the number of "rest nears." On the following Tuesday, the pair mated. But he does readily admit that his method is not foolproof.

When it comes to their charismatic megafauna, Beck says, zoo officials are reluctant to make drastic moves, but he hopes his analysis of the characteristics of gorilla compatibility will give curators the tools they need to make important decisions. To refine and extend these insights, Beck has collected complete biographies of every captive gorilla in North America and has searched these records for the correlates of sexual and parental success. The critical ingredient is simple: a gorilla infant must have rich social experience with other gorillas in the first eighteen months of life.

This kind of multipronged research approach—the careful examination of field data, hands-on physiological inspection, and observation of exhibit animals—is more and more the norm at the zoo. Indeed, one can think of the zoo as a wide-ranging zoological research institute, motivated chiefly but not solely by the pragmatic needs of the animals in its care, with an urgent curiosity about literally every aspect of animals and their natural and human-made habitats. The zoo is one of the few places in the world where understanding of our fellow creatures on the planet is pursued at all levels from the molecular to the whole animal, where a species' evolutionary history is attended to as well as its future. Zoos want to know about animals per se—a respectful sort of inquiry. If insights emerge that are directly helpful to humans, that's fine. But these are animal people.

Virtually everyone gets into the act. The giant panda keepers have engaged in a project to collect from all zoos that have giant pandas detailed information on weight plotted against age for these animals—baseline data that simply hasn't been collected up until now. In the nutrition laboratory, scientists reflected on the fact that many zoo animals need crickets in their diet. No one had ever, it seems, thought to analyze crickets for their protein content: it is now being done.

The National Zoo's research output is unparalleled by any other zoo in the world and far more varied. Some of it appears to be almost purely theoretical, and one might wonder why with all of the urgencies of caring for a living collection the zoo would devote some of its valuable time and money to matters that do not have an immediately realizable application. One answer is that all knowledge of life is valuable, and in a world that remains so full of mystery, it would be foolhardy to insist that an answer to a purely theoretical question will not lead to a highly practical benefit. Curators at zoos are generally evaluated as to job performance by how well they have managed the creatures in their care and by various personnel considerations. At the National Zoo the above criteria apply, but another important factor is the curator's scientific output and quality. In short, they are evaluated as Smithsonian scientists as well as zoo people.

As Christen Wemmer says, "Zoos used to be good old boy institutions where people worked their way up from keeper." This of course

South American mouse opossums are among the many little-known mammals being studied for the first time at the National Zoo. Unusual for marsupials, these opossums lack a pouch in which to carry their young.

151

Though devoted to the study of rare and exotic species, zoo scientists also conduct field studies of common North American animals like white-tailed deer and Virginia opossums.

can still occur and does, "but zoos have now been invaded by scholarly young turks." The academic aura permeating the Rock Creek and Front Royal installations is the chief distinguishing characteristic of the new zoo.

The desire to answer what may seem a minor scientific question can lead, serendipitously, to profound results. Katherine Ralls did not set out to explore inbreeding; she was merely hoping to develop some insight into parent-child relationships among Dorcas gazelles. When she began studying the records, she perceived the effects of inbreeding, and the result was a major revolution in the way zoos do business.

The surprising, even shameful, fact is the tremendous amount we simply don't know about a lot of animals—even now so late in the twentieth century. Miles Roberts, curator of the zoo's research collection and inhabitor of a pleasantly cluttered office in the animal hospital building, points out that in South America there are mammals yet to be identified. One of Roberts's tasks (he is also the red panda Species Survival Plan coordinator) is to describe the basic biology of little known animals: their life histories, including such matters as gestation periods and the size of litters.

For example, there are about eighty species of possums in South America and little is known about most of them. It takes about five years to obtain enough litters to develop basic data of the sort Roberts seeks, and he hopes over the next several years to go through these species systematically. Of course he can't do them all. Instead he plans to pick representative ones: tiny, medium-sized, and large. He will also select across ecological gradients: possums that live in dry or wet or seasonal areas. And he'll choose from dietary categories: insect, fruit, fish, and mixed diets. At least a general picture of possumhood will emerge.

He, or other field workers, after having observed the animal's lifestyles in the wild will remove them to the zoo's research collection for continuing observation. Many aspects of animal life cannot practically be studied in the wild. "Females with babies," Roberts points out, "don't trap well."

Having established founding colonies of the possums, Roberts will collect the data and produce biological profiles of them. Then, in many cases he will ship some of the founders' descendants to other institutions accompanied by what are called "protocols." A protocol is essentially an operator's manual for maintaining and breeding a given species. Satisfying the requirements of the species takes considerable inventiveness, as in the case of the Western tarsier from Borneo, which Roberts and his colleagues have successfully bred in captivity—only the second known time this has occurred.

The Western tarsier is among what Roberts has called the "Not Really Rare, Semicharismatic Microvertebrates." It and the two other tarsier species are unique among primates in being exclusively carnivorous; they are nocturnal animals, also a rarity among primates, and their amazingly large eyes are a testimony to this. Typically they cling to trees with their long fingers and toes, and turning their heads up to 180 degrees they leap from trunk to trunk in pursuit of insect prey. They are called ghost monkeys by native peoples because, as Roberts says, they "appear and disappear noiselessly as if turned on and off by a switch."

Little is known of the natural history of these elusive animals in the wild, and captive studies have been few for the very reason that zoos have rarely succeeded in maintaining them for very long. Consequently, in the 1960s and 1970s none were on exhibit in the United States. In 1983, with the collaboration of Patricia Wright of the Duke University Primate Center in Durham, North Carolina, Roberts obtained two pairs from the wild. Wright mist-netted the animals and put them in a wire cage on the spot for two weeks to acclimatize them to captivity. Those not responding well to their new conditions were released. Then she brought them to the United States in small cages in the passenger section of an airplane, the cargo area being too cool and dry for the animals; evidently other attempts to bring tarsiers back alive have failed because this precaution was not taken.

The zoo's tarsiers were given cages with plenty of bamboo and dowels for their acrobatic proclivities, a constant temperature of about eighty degrees, and humidity of about sixty-five percent. Incandescent bulbs provided daytime illumination and a twenty-watt blue bulb provided moonlight. Roberts's staff experimented with a variety of live food from lizards to cockroaches, but the tarsiers preferred crickets almost exclusively. Crickets, it had been found, lack certain vitamins and trace minerals. One can dust crickets with the needed supplement, but this only works with dead crickets, which tarsiers won't eat. Live crickets groom most of the supplement off almost immediately. Answer: feed the crickets the needed supplement. They do not incorporate it into their own bodily tissues so it goes straight to the tarsiers. Each tarsier eats about two hundred crickets a week.

Like most wild animals, the tarsiers had parasites on arrival, but the animals were judged to be too delicate to worm via tubing. Using crickets as unwitting carriers of the medication seemed unreliable. So Roberts's group mixed the wormer with a thick palatable paste and, while the tarsiers were asleep, applied it with a tongue depressor to the animals' thighs. Upon waking, the tarsiers, being fastidious about cleanliness, licked the annoying paste off.

The tarsiers, the researchers found, have an exceptionally long gestation period for so small an animal—six months—and shortly before birth the mother becomes intolerant of her mate. In one case, before this was perceived, a father killed its infant. The cages were quickly modified so that the females can separate themselves from the males when they feel the need.

With such insights, the protocol for these animals is complete and, as Roberts says, "There is no reason to believe that any zoo willing to invest the time and money couldn't maintain tarsiers." The benefits of this sort of research can extend far beyond the needs of zoos. Scientists studying human embryology require the use of research animals, and one of the best kinds of animal for such research are marsupials because the young are essentially born outside the mother's body. Thus, the embryologist can use noninvasive techniques for observing

The Western tarsier, native only to the southeast Asian islands of Borneo, Sumatra, and Bangka, also occupies a comfortable arboreal habitat in a zoo enclosure.

such things as which parts of the body develop at which rates. One of Roberts's protocols, on the marsupial *Monodelphis*, led to that animal becoming a standard laboratory animal for such research. While Roberts has the tenderest feelings for "his" animals, he is well aware that certain kinds of medical research are better carried out on a strain of a captive animal than on, say, one's child.

Protocols are a main part of the business upstairs in the Reptile House. For example, anyone who wants to raise green pythons will be interested in the protocols of keeper Trooper Walsh. Over the years he has kept many kinds of pythons both in his home, before he began working for the zoo, and at the Reptile House. He has witnessed the laying of hundreds of clutches of python eggs, including more than twenty green tree python clutches. In the process he has made discoveries that will aid in husbandry and captive breeding of these snakes. For instance, a keeper likes to know when a female python is gravid because, among other things, she needs a constantly warm environment. One way to identify a gravid female is by what Walsh calls the "deflated head appearance," a situation in which the sides of the normally bulbous head come to look sunken. Just what causes this remains unknown; Walsh speculates that it may have something to do with a change in circulation to let greater blood supplies reach the oviducts.

Keepers are also called upon to conduct particular experiments that bear on practical matters. There was some concern that handling reptile eggs might lower their chances of hatching. Experiments with the eggs of a tortoise, a lizard, and two snakes showed that handling the eggs once a week had no effect at all on hatching. Likewise, there was the idea that similar to some fish, reptiles in small enclosures would grow less than those in larger enclosures. A keeper-run experiment with corn snakes over a period of three years eliminated that myth.

Dale Marcellini, curator of reptiles, speaks with a mixture of amusement and awe of the talents of another reptile keeper, Cecilia Chang, and her frog explosion. He opens the door to a holding room and says, "Welcome to Frog City." Tank after tank is studded with arrays of what seem to be opalescent jade: Australian tree frogs. Chang has a special talent for breeding such creatures and her success caught Marcellini off guard. "When you've got a success with amphibians, you've really got a success." Chang wants to breed everything, and Marcellini, delighted with her prowess, nonetheless speaks with conviction about the need for species selection planning and annual reviews lest the Reptile House experience the Sorcerer's Apprentice Syndrome. What does one do with a surplus of Australian tree frogs? One plan is to trade some to a university in return for letting Chang attend a special course in amphibian captive breeding!

Marcellini spends part of each year in the field researching the ecology and behavior of little-known reptiles. On several occasions he has worked in Cuba, helping to delineate the nature of that island's reptilian fauna. Once field studies have been completed, he sometimes collects specimens and brings them back to the zoo. There the classic mode of experiment is to introduce males and females and observe how they communicate and how they settle in with each other. Cur-

(Below) Green tree pythons in the process of hatching.

(Right) Rain frogs breed in dense aggregations.

rently he is entranced with some New Zealand geckos that inhabit holding cages near a row of windows in the upstairs quarters of the Reptile House. They are Auckland green geckos, though some of them are yellow (the only yellow lizards known), and they appear to be highly social. They like low temperatures; it rarely gets above eighty degrees on the north island of New Zealand where they live—and they remain perfectly active in the window cages where it is quite cool. "This is a different lifestyle from that of any other lizard I know," says Marcellini.

Evidently these geckos are extremely hard to find. "They're green, they're supposedly diurnal, and they're supposed to live on plants. They should be easy to find, but they aren't." In one instance thirty-one members of a New Zealand herpetological organization fanned out and spent hours looking for this species. They spotted only two. The geckos live in areas where there is a monoculture of brushfields, like the California coastal chaparral. This is an odd place for a lizard, since most prefer a varied edge habitat. As Marcellini admits, "They're just curious animals."

One form of animal behavior into which the zoo has not conducted any special research is the restlessness of zoologists. About once a year the researchers get a peculiar look in the eye and a certain kind of inner tremor. Before long, they must go off to the field, or even among so basically good-natured a group, there might develop a certain amount of social dysfunction. Indeed, combining field studies with observation of captive members of the same species is usual at the zoo. The value of this dual approach is well illustrated by studies of the maned wolf.

In 1978 James Dietz (who was later to welcome the tamarins back to Brazil) began a two-year field study of this South American wolf. Though it is prized in zoos and endangered throughout its range, little was known of its social behavior or ecology largely because it is timid and secretive. A researcher is unlikely to see much of maned wolves. Dietz designed a special box trap to safely catch them and placed several in a Brazilian park called Serra da Canastra. The goal was to place a collar on each maned wolf resident in the park and by means of a radio transmitter on the collar track the whereabouts and activity level of the wolves year-round. In addition, there were various other indirect ways to garner data about the wolves, including analysis of the animals' droppings.

Via radiotelemetry and actual observations, Dietz determined that there were three distinct home ranges for the wolves within the study area. It became apparent from their movements that pairs of wolves shared ranges. Indeed, it appeared that these wolves formed pair bonds, male and female, displaying facultative monogamy. The two remain associated but for the most part spend practically no time with each other. Such an insight would, of course, be valuable for managers of captive populations of this creature, but the evidence for it, from radio signals, was essentially circumstantial, however compelling.

Scientists working with satellite photographs have a term called

Native to South American grasslands, the maned wolf is largely solitary, but males and females form loose monogamous pair bonds.

"ground truth." They will look at a photograph and make certain assumptions about terrain and soil type from the difference between various shades of color on the photograph. In a new situation, they will send people to the spot to confirm that a particular color in the photograph indeed means a certain kind of soil. In zoological research, the process is reversed. The "ground truth" of a field observation can be confirmed by studying captive populations. This is what Dietz did, observing the wolves at the zoo's Conservation and Research Center during the breeding and postweaning seasons over a period of eighteen months.

Hidden in the little tower that rises over the maned wolf pens, Dietz would watch for four hours at a stretch, noting the precise whereabouts of each member of the pair under study. From these observations, he was able to confirm the pair bonding and to demonstrate that there is a certain division of labor wherein the female raises and protects the young primarily alone, while the male patrols and defends the boundary of their mutual territory. Prior to these studies, maned wolves had normally been kept separate from the opposite sex except at breeding time; now they are kept as pairs and their chances of surviving in captivity are increased.

Matters do not always work out so neatly. Several years back, Wemmer assuaged a bout of oncoming fieldworker's syndrome by journeying to Sulawesi (formerly the Celebes) in Indonesia. There a very rare civet, the Sulawesi palm civet, one of the least-known carnivores in the world, lives its elusive life. Wemmer and Dick Watling, an associate employed by the World Wildlife Fund–Indonesia, assembled a considerable amount of data about this animal—for example, the means by which it managed to coexist with the more common Malay civet and the fact that it was more widespread than was previously thought. They collected a mating pair with a view to starting a captive population at Front Royal. At the last moment, however, officials in Sulawesi reversed themselves and denied Wemmer permission to take the captives home. They were instead removed to the local zoo which, unhappily, did not have the necessary facilities. The animals died.

"That's the way it goes sometimes," says Wemmer, shaking his head. "Well, at least we know a little more about them, we know they aren't especially endangered. . . ."

It is heartening in a time of the equalization of the sexes to find that this benevolent program has analogues among other animals, even among that aggressive and piratical creature, the sea gull. Anyone who has had a picnic on the beach has seen the argumentative ways in which gulls hassle each other over who gets the crust of the sandwich. Anyone who throws bread repeatedly to the gulls sees the pattern of dominance emerge. One gull, or a few, chase the others away and get the food. Gulls are very expressive and have a number of ways of signifying dominance or submission: vocal signals, postures, and actual attacks, ranging from running at each other to prolonged pecking. This is a relatively standard means of resolving conflict in the animal world; each species has its own set of signals. Studying the vocalizations of birds and other animals, zoo ornithologist Eugene Morton has found that there is a similar "grammar" among all mammals and birds, and by decoding it one can close in on an understanding of the motivation of the animal at any given moment. Generally a high sound means submission or fear or a babylike need for affection, like the call of the bullied golden lion tamarin.

One of Morton's students, Judith Hand, noting the fact that gulls form male and female pair bonds, wondered how a pair resolved conflicts over such matters as food and the task of incubating the eggs. Both parents incubate the eggs: who is the one to decide who will sit on the nest? Hand studied three species of gulls in the wild and one species, silver gulls, in the Bird House at the National Zoo. After months of meticulous observation, she was able to classify the various behaviors of the gulls and understand their structural role in conflict resolution. It appears that gull pairs practice an egalitarian method of conflict resolution. They share equally a large piece of food, and when something small turns up, the first of the pair to get there eats it: there is no threat from the other. They both behave as if they felt the other had equal rights. And the choice of who gets to sit on the nest is determined by a complex "conversation" consisting of "choking" and head tossing and other signals by which the "on" gull either requests relief or exhibits a determination to stay on. Meanwhile, the "off" gull will similarly ask to get on or suggest it wants to remain off, the intensity of the mutual signaling eventually leading to a decision.

There is some question whether such communication is always "honest"—that is, whether one gull may put on the dog a bit in order to manipulate the behavior of its mate, or whether the signaling is a precise and unalterable expression of the gull's true motivation.

Another sea gull activity suggests that these birds aren't altogether straightforward. Various people have noted that often when one gull goes after a piece of food, pursued by the others, it will emit a high call, as if signaling fear—which it clearly is not doing. Morton suggests that the gull may be trying to make the other gulls think there is a predator around so that they will hesitate, giving the signaling gull a better shot at the morsel.

At any rate, it is believed that most of these vocal signals are "honest," and Morton takes the matter several steps further, leading him eventually to a possible explanation of how human speech evolved. Take the case of a mother goose sitting on her eggs who is confronted by a fox. The chances are that she experiences two feelings at the same time: a desire to flee and a desire to protect her eggs. What she does is to get into a threatening posture, head down and wings slightly

Parental care falls primarily to the female in maned wolf pairs, although males have been observed to feed and otherwise contribute to the survival of their young.

raised, and she hisses. The hiss is a nonvocal sound. If, Morton theorized, she made a vocal sound it would be to her disadvantage. First of all, because she really does want to flee with one part of her mind, she cannot "lie" and give out a harsh low vocal sound that in all birds and mammals signifies aggression. And if she did make a vocal sound, because of her desire to flee, it might well come out high-pitched, giving the fox the idea that she is submitting. The hiss, being nonvocal, masks the goose's feelings. In encounters among all animals and birds, Morton suggests, the wide variety of clicks, hisses, and other nonvocal sounds serve to disguise dangerous or inappropriate feelings, which can, in the right circumstances, be expressed vocally along the continuum of high-pitched fear to low and harsh aggression.

One of the things, Morton points out, that distinguishes human speech is that somewhere along the evolutionary way humans combined both kinds of communication into one. The pitch of vocal sounds, their intensity and other characteristics, can convey considerable information as to gender, emotional state, and so forth—just as among animals. This is called paralanguage, and it includes crying and laughing as well. But in pronouncing as part of our speech such sounds as those called for by the letters t and k, humans uniquely combine nonvocal and vocal sounds into one language. Why?

Unless there is specific evidence in favor of it, evolutionary biologists do not believe that such things as communicatory methods arise de novo in each species. The expressive sound symbolism that is common in birds and mammals must have been extant in some prototypical mode in their ancestors, the reptiles, and there is evidence that dinosaurs were far more expressive than today's reptiles. Something of this system must have been present in those mammals that became human. So what advantage would protohominids have gained by combining vocal sounds, which express emotion, with nonvocal sounds, which in other species mask emotion?

Morton suggests that the answer is connected with inbreeding and outbreeding. Bands of protohominids, like their apelike ancestors, needed some mechanism for splitting off certain members to join other bands, as among gorillas. Whether it was males or females who left the band, there might have been some advantage for these highly communicative creatures when they found themselves among a new band to communicate in a way that hid any signs of fear or anger.

Going yet further, Morton notes that human children can learn any language known on earth with relative ease. But after puberty, their facility for foreign languages generally diminishes. What evolutionary advantage—scientists call it "inclusive fitness"—was to be gained by a deterioration in language-learning ability? An individual joining a new band who had difficulty in learning the language perfectly would have an accent, seem foreign, and therefore be an especially desirable mate. This, naturally, would provide a hedge against inbreeding.

So here among the hundreds of research projects and experiments conducted at the National Zoo, we find what might be totally unexpected: an ornithologist shedding light on the evolution of human speech. That's even more startling than seeing scimitar-horned oryxes in a grassy pasture in Virginia.

Equally fascinating to artists, amateur naturalists, and practitioners of "pure" scientific research, the biology of birds—from their breeding behavior to their methods of communication—continues to be a major focus of zoo researchers.

SACRED GROVES

About three centuries before the birth of Christ, Prince Mahinda arrived in the land now known as Sri Lanka with the hope of proselytizing the local people to Buddhism, a relatively new religion that had originated in what is now Nepal and spread across the Asian continent. It is reported that he chose for the topic of his first sermon the management of wildlife, and we can guess that elephants figured in his sermon, being then as now the largest land mammals. Today Buddhists still contemplate the complicated relationship between elephants and humans, and they have recently been joined by the World Bank and the Agency for International Development. Another key interlocutor in the affairs of elephants and humans has in the past two decades been the National Zoo. The four do not, it turns out, make strange bedfellows.

Over the millennia, elephants were widely admired throughout their Asian habitat and many of them were trained, becoming in a sense partners with humans. They were, and still are, used for transportation and labor. There are few more efficient ways even today to log a forest selectively than with elephants. And they were and still are featured in religious ceremonies and festivals as quasi-religious beings. Also, throughout the millennia, elephants have raided agricultural lands, to the lasting frustration of farmers, especially Buddhist farmers, who regard the taking of any life as a grave transgression.

In Sri Lanka (then Ceylon) during the nineteenth century, reverence for the elephant was somewhat overridden by the world view of the imperial British, who paid rewards for the destruction of 5,500 elephants, nearly half of the estimated population. One man, a Major Rogers, claimed the grisly distinction of having dispatched 1,100 elephants himself. In recent times, Asian elephant deaths have been about equally the result of habitat destruction and crop protection. The population—now restricted to the drier zones of the country—is estimated to be some 2,500 animals.

In the late 1960s it was evident to officials at the National Zoo—and, in particular, to John Eisenberg, then resident scientist—that increasing development of Sri Lankan land for agricultural purposes was eliminating elephant habitat and at the same time leading to more and more depredations of farmland, resulting in more losses of elephants to cropland defense: a double bind. Eisenberg and his colleagues, George McKay and Fred Kurt, undertook an extensive field study of the Ceylon elephant, its habitat, and, chiefly, its social behavior—for from knowledge of how elephants organize their lives might come insights into how to manage more properly our increasingly troubled relationships with them. The foresight of this expedition is remarkable. Nearly two decades later, the project that had its beginnings almost purely as an investigation of elephant behavior and ecology is paying dividends in management practices that may well save the elephant in Sri Lanka. The venerability of the study is brought home by the fact that the inaugural issue of *Smithsonian* magazine in April 1970 carried on its cover a photograph of Sri Lankan elephants taken during the early years of the study. Nearly two hundred monthly issues of the magazine later, the zoo is still actively engaged with elephants in Sri Lanka.

A typical herd of elephants, it was found by the Eisenberg team, consists of mostly females—a matriarch and other, usually related females, including some young ones, as well as a few young males: sometimes as many as thirty animals in all. Young males are evicted from the herd before they reach maturity and spend most of the rest of their lives either alone or with loosely defined groups of other males, except during breeding times when they tend to seek out estrous females. The cow herd has been called the repository of traditional knowledge among elephants, the needed society in which the young learn about reproduction, child rearing, foods, and the proper places to travel. And travel they do. In the dry season of the year they will congregate near permanent sources of water; in the wetter season, they migrate in smaller bands in quest of more nutritionally rich fodder, grass being an important component of their diet. They learn the whereabouts of—and regularly trek to—the sites of mineral licks.

The destruction of elephant habitat, of course, diminishes the amount of land available for elephant use, but it can also block traditional routes linking separate sections of elephants' extensive home ranges. Herds can become "pocketed" in a small area of habitat surrounded by agricultural lands. The result is predictable: they raid crops.

Among the many things the Eisenberg research team turned up was

The appearance of elephants in Asian art is just one manifestation of the close relationship between people and elephants that permeates Asian culture. Symbolized by the intense, near-mystical bond between a mahout and the elephants he works, this relationship combines reverence and respect for elephants with the need to manage and control some elephants for human uses. But throughout Asia, elephants and people are today coming increasingly into conflict as people tame the wilderness habitats of elephants and other wildlife. Nepal's Chitwan Valley, for instance, was sparsely settled until malaria was brought under control with DDT in the 1960s and people flocked to this valley in the outermost ranges of the Himalayas. Ironically, even to study the problems requires the use of elephants. Only on the backs of domestic elephants could National Zoo scientists move and observe wildlife in the tall grasses—up to twenty-five feet high—and sal forest of Chitwan.

As elephant habitat and, consequently, elephant numbers decline, concern grows both about the survival of elephants in the wild and the supply of elephants for work. Extremely difficult to breed in captivity, wild elephants are often captured when they are young. Young, tractable animals are most amenable to training and eventually will become productive workers, primarily in logging and other tasks where their enormous strength and durability in rough terrain still beat the best equipment modern technology has to offer. Trained elephants also serve science. National Zoo scientists have been able to study the conservation genetics of Asian elephants in Sri Lanka and elsewhere because they can easily collect blood samples from the ears of trained elephants for analysis.

Rudy Rudran. Rudran, after working with the Smithsonian scientists for several years, was asked to produce an environmental impact statement for the Sri Lankan government, making recommendations for lessening a massive development scheme's impact not only on elephants but on other endangered species such as the leopard and the crocodile. There would be development, to be sure, and just as inevitable was crop devastation by elephants, if history was any indication. In 1977 alone, in teak plantations of some 4,500 acres, elephants accounted for losses of $75 million in future revenues. Of many environmental concerns Rudran addressed, one was how to lessen the impact of farms on elephants and elephants on farms.

One of the problems, Rudran knew, is that elephants seem to like edges, particularly edges of forests, for example, that are bordered by grassland. Such areas provide a greater variety of nutritious fodder. If a development creates a nice edge between forest and a tasty food-crop, the elephants will revel in it.

In the vast area where the rapid agricultural development was planned, there were already a few reserves set aside for wildlife. Rudran's impact statement, delivered in 1980, recommended that these be enlarged and upgraded, that four new reserves be established, and that a jungle corridor between several of them be maintained to take account of the elephant's migratory traditions. These recommendations were, of course, only some among a large array of suggestions made in the document covering such issues as different kinds of habitat, canal building, conservation education, and the upgrading of wildlife management expertise within the government.

The development plans and the environmental impact statement moved gradually through the various Sri Lankan ministries, but the jungle corridor was determined to be an extravagance, along with several of the recommended refuges. Eventually a proposal was made to the World Bank to help finance the project. Following standard practice, the World Bank dispatched the newly received proposal for expert commentary, and it soon wound up in the zoo's former administration building called Holt House on the desk of none other than Rudran. Subsequently, Rudran explained in his soft voice, the World Bank demanded an environmental plan of action before it would fund the development project. The four parks have now been replaced in the plan.

The World Bank soon realized that it was engaged in a number of projects around the tropics that involved elephants and called upon the National Zoo to provide guidance. In 1984, John Seidensticker, who had worked with Rudran on the environmental evaluation in Sri Lanka as a field biologist and who is now a mammals curator at the zoo, joined in what may have been the oddest colloquium ever sponsored by the World Bank. His message was that planners should deliberately make places that are good for elephants and places where elephants are uncomfortable, pointing out that "where an elephant is determined it usually succeeds." Obstacles are of little use: elephants will fill in steep-sided ditches with mud, using their feet. Ivory tusks don't conduct electricity, so if an elephant doesn't push a tree over an electric fence, it will simply knock down the fence itself. Seiden-

In Sri Lanka's Mahaveli region, development and elephants meet head on. Fueled by construction of a series of dams, croplands are replacing what was once prime elephant habitat. Elephants have responded by raiding farms and destroying crops; to their dismay, farmers find themselves threatened by animals they hold in great esteem. Development has also created a novel hazard for elephants: Baby elephants fall into wells they are helpless to escape from without human intervention. Most of the babies in Sri Lanka's elephant orphanage were rescued from wells. Working with the government of Sri Lanka, the Agency for International Development, the World Bank, and other agencies, National Zoo elephant experts helped ensure that buffer zones—areas between forest and cropland where wild elephants can graze without conflict with people—were included in the Mahaveli development scheme.

Perhaps because of the National Zoo's century-old commitment to caring for both the animals in its collection and the people who come to see them, zoo field researchers bring a unique perspective to wildlife conservation. All recognize the deep emotional bond between people and animals—a bond that ensures the success of conservation efforts as long as the basic needs of people can also be met. In Nepal, for instance, zoo scientists determined that collecting thatch grass was not detrimental to the wildlife in the Royal Chitwan National Park. Now once a year villagers are permitted to collect this essential roofing material in the park, which is the only source of thatch grass for many people living in the valley. As a result, people respect the park's boundaries and rules the rest of the year. In Sri Lanka, zoo scientists provide advice to reduce conflicts between people and elephants and between development and conservation, knowing that wildlife conservation is not only compatible with long-term economic prosperity, but essential to it.

sticker encouraged planners to forget features that are "essentially walls intended to challenge elephants," but to concentrate instead on boundaries having "zero appeal." A buffer zone between forest and farmland that consists of grasslands severely overgrazed by livestock will discourage elephants from leaving the forest. The main point was that it is more cost-effective, from the planner's standpoint, to manage elephants in and near project areas from the very beginning of the program. But it is not only planners and global movers and shakers who have a stake in such management. "If you don't take elephants seriously," Rudran says, "it will hurt the rural people. It's their paddy that will get hammered."

Rudran has offered a plan for handling the growing elephant-human conflict in his native land. First, elephants that do damage crops should be captured—not shot by the locals. In capturing a herd, Rudran points out, it is important to capture the matriarch first: without her, the rest slow down. On the other hand, if a young elephant in a herd is captured first, the elders will often retaliate, endangering human lives, or flee, making capture all the more unlikely. Captured herds can be relocated as intact social units (if there is room elsewhere for them) or sold at auction (with the proceeds of the sale benefiting the local community) and domesticated for use as "monitor" animals (animals that help in capture operations) in national parks or in the lumbering industry. Captive breeding of such animals could and should be attempted, though it is difficult and dangerous. Generally, breeding elephants calls for elaborate and expensive equipment, such as mammoth holding cages to restrain bulls in musth.

Widespread education programs in Sri Lanka would reinforce the notion of the economic rewards that could accrue to local communities under this strategy, so farmers would be more likely to call the authorities and have the interlopers captured rather than—in lonely exasperation—open fire. The strategy Rudran proposes is one that links economic development and human needs to the goals of conservation. He doesn't expect that this would save all the elephants involved: some would surely be lost in the capture process. But it would democratize the conservation effort and provide the people with a social impetus to overcome the problem and solve what Rudran sees as an "underlying cultural dilemma that is perhaps more serious than the apparent losses through crop damage." It is not within the religious traditions of Sri Lanka to shoot an elephant, and Rudran's plan would relieve his countrymen of this moral burden. It would help Sri Lanka contend "with the pangs of economic growth and development without being pushed into moral or cultural bankruptcy. This gain is priceless."

It may not be necessary to emphasize that lecturing the World Bank on the behavior of elephants and protecting the economic and moral health of farmers are hardly usual tasks for a zoo. Nor have scientists traditionally put much stock in religious beliefs or found it necessary to be international diplomats. But in the new zoo, there is a recognition that in a game one hopes will be of indefinite duration, it is best if all the players win.

For several generations, biologists have migrated with nearly the regularity of birds to an island in the Gatun Lake that was created when the Panama Canal was built. The island is Barro Colorado, host to the Smithsonian Tropical Research Institute. It is fair to say that this installation is the most productive source of knowledge about tropical biology anywhere in the world. But so rich are tropical ecosystems that most of their flora and fauna, even from the standpoint of taxonomy and natural history, remains unknown—and this at a time when tropical ecosystems are falling to human invasion and desecration worldwide at a rate that has led some observers to predict the end of the tropical rain forest sometime in the next century.

In the 1970s zoo officials recognized not only the urgency for more tropical research, but the need to find an area where a biological data base could be developed for comparison to the information gathered at Barro Colorado. Venezuela was selected because of its diverse fauna—much like Panama's, although the forest habitats are quite different—and because there had been very few large-scale concentrated formal investigations anywhere on the South American mainland.

In Venezuela were howler monkeys, capuchin monkeys, iguanas, various carnivores, anteaters, and birds that were common also to Panama. The zoo found nearly ideal circumstances for carrying out its studies in the seventies, thanks to the dream of a man named Tomas Blohm. Blohm is a wealthy businessman and cattle rancher with a passion for wildlife. His 27,000-hectare cattle ranch located along the Guarico River is called Hato Masaguaral. On his ranch there is canopy forest in places but mostly habitat called llanos, characterized by short-statured forests alternating with savannah. Seasonally, the region is either arid or subject to flooding; during the dry season from December to April, visibility for animal observations is excellent. Blohm has long welcomed scientists to study wildlife. He prevents hunting on his ranch and contributed to the building of housing facilities for the Smithsonian scientists: his ranch is one of the most fertile sources of tropical biology studies in South America. Some 150 scientists from fifteen countries have pursued long- and short-term research projects there in what is called the Venezuela Project.

It was at Masaguaral that zoo scientists were able to elaborate the role of infanticide in red howler monkeys—a case where a new male takes over a band and kills the young of the previous male, either to clear the band of paternal genes other than his own or to eliminate competition for food in times of scarcity so that his offspring will thrive. (While these and other studies were made chiefly in the spirit of pure science, it is not difficult to see the implications of the infanticide discoveries for those maintaining captive populations of these animals.)

It was apparent before the project began that the generally held notion that tropical ecosystems are stable is not necessarily true. Not only are there distinct seasonal changes for the animals to cope with, but also a fairly dynamic succession of plant life. How species adapt to these environmental fluctuations became a major focus of the project.

One such adaptation is the unique mating system of the snail kite, a tropical hawk also found in south Florida, where it used to be called the Everglade kite. Recently, the American Ornithological Union renamed it, taking into account its specialized habit of feeding on freshwater snails. In the early 1980s Steven Beissinger, a zoo research associate, discovered among the endangered Florida population of the kites that in times when snails are plentiful, either parent may desert its mate when the young are only halfway raised, sometimes to find another mate and nest again, behavior not typical of any other vertebrate. Was it practiced by the Venezuelan snail kite as well? Beissinger spent six months in 1985 trying to find out. He located fifty nests in the vicinity of Masaguaral: most of them failed. This is also common in the Florida population—the result of predation by other raptors and snakes as well as storm winds—but the chief cause in Venezuela appears to be predation: there are few storms there. In eight of nine successful nests, Beissinger observed that mates did desert, leaving a single parent to mind the fledglings for some two to three weeks. The logic of this behavior is clear. If the deserter finds another mate it can double its annual brood. And with the wonderful serendipity that often occurs in fieldwork, Beissinger was able to confirm another suspicion that may give pause to the name-changers at the American Ornithological Union. Snail kites also eat crabs.

One way scientists gauge the effectiveness of a program such as the Smithsonian's Venezuela Project is to add up the number of scientific publications and presentations that have resulted, the theory being that only valuable research results are likely to be published. In its first five years, the project proved itself to be an overwhelming suc-

Iguanas and red howler monkeys are among the many diverse species National Zoo scientists track in the llanos of Venezuela. Grasslands dominate the llanos, but the arboreal howler monkeys survive in small patches of low forest sprinkled amid the savannas and in gallery forests along rivers.

Throughout the New World tropics, clearing forests for cattle ranching threatens wildlife. But Tomas Blohm's cattle ranch provides a haven for wild animals and for the National Zoo scientists who study them. Blohm has won international acclaim for his conservation efforts in Venezuela.

Leaf-eating hoatzin inhabit the forested banks of rivers and streams of Venezuela, where they build twig and stick nests on branches that may overhang the water. Nestling hoatzin swim with ease and even dive into the water to escape predators.

cess by this measure at a total cost in Smithsonian research funds of approximately $200,000. This is some of the most cost-effective science one can find: the same amount of money over the same period of time would buy a fraction of the equipment necessary to maintain an astronomical telescope or would pay the salary of an assistant manager at a fast-food hamburger store, which is indirectly complicit in the transformation of tropical rain forests into cattle ranches. Of course, all this research has benefited enormously from the generosity of Blohm, who recently spent a very large sum to acquire additional lands for the study area.

Among the recent research projects at Masaguaral, one particularly illustrates the value of cross-disciplinary studies in such a place. On the ranch there is a bird, the hoatzin, that eats leaves (it is what scientists call an obligate folivore.) An ornithologist from the New York Zoological Society, Stuart Strahl, in collaboration with the zoo's Eugene Morton, is researching the dietary ecology of this bird, including a nutrient analysis of the leaves it feeds on. At the same time the zoo's nutritionist, Olav Oftedal, is probing feeding habits of red howler monkeys, who not only are folivorous, but also eat some of the same plants as the hoatzin. The two studies, progressing simultaneously, pose a unique opportunity to answer a question of importance to ecological theory—how two altogether unrelated species with different lifestyles and even different gut anatomy can share this food niche and deal in their different ways with the digestive and nutritive problems of folivory. The knowledge gained could be of prime importance to zoos with captive primates that are folivorous (such as gorillas), which often have serious dietary problems.

When John Seidensticker, fresh from several years of studying mountain lions in the American West, arrived in Nepal's Royal Chitwan National Park in late January 1973, he decided not to spend his first night indoors in the shelter used by the park guards. Instead he chose to stretch out on a river bank and enjoy what seemed to him a bit of heaven. During the night he heard the sounds of various kinds of deer—warning calls that started off to his right and continued in a semicircle around to his left. The deer were alerting each other to the presence of a tiger. Then the tiger roared back. Reminiscing about that night recently, Seidensticker smiled and said he probably would not sleep out alone like that in Chitwan again if he had the chance, but that first experience convinced him that Chitwan was the study site he sought. He and numerous other researchers have learned a great deal about the tiger since that night in 1973 when the Smithsonian–Nepal Tiger Ecology Project got underway.

The project almost didn't begin at all. It had its origins in 1967 when S. Dillon Ripley, then secretary of the Smithsonian, startled members of the Bombay Natural History Society by saying that he believed the tiger would be extinct in twenty-five years. The reasons were poaching, legalized hunting (to attract tourist income), and lax management in parks and preserves. Many people in India did not take kindly to this commentary from what they felt was a well-intentioned but misguided foreigner, but a number of Indian conservationists shared Ri-

pley's view. Two years later, at a meeting of the International Union for the Conservation of Nature and Natural Resources in New Delhi, the tiger's plight was discussed and the IUCN called on all the nations of Southeast Asia to declare a moratorium on hunting these big cats. An accurate census of the tiger population was requested and was subsequently performed by the New Delhi Zoo. There were, it turned out, only 2,500 tigers in India, drastically down from the 40,000 animals estimated at the turn of the century, even from the 4,000 estimated in 1965. In 1971 the Indian government organized a tiger project to halt the decline, and the following year the World Wildlife Fund International announced a million dollar "Operation Tiger" designed to save the tiger in India and the rest of Southeast Asia.

Ripley and others at the Smithsonian believed that it would require much more than the traditional measures of strict enforcement of regulations and of public education. It would take a detailed knowledge of tiger ecology. Ripley had offered the services of the Smithsonian to the Indian government as early as 1969. There had been few in-depth studies of any large carnivores; what few had been done were chiefly in North America where a new technology was emerging: radio tracking. The Indian government, however, remained cool to the Smithsonian's repeated offers to cooperate, and the World Wildlife Fund International did not believe that a scientific study was necessary.

In 1972 a chance meeting occurred at a world conference on national parks held in the United States. While the Indian delegation remained unenthusiastic about scientific collaboration, a Smithsonian official and John Seidensticker met a Nepali delegation that seemed far more receptive to the idea. Seidensticker was invited to Nepal and with Kirti Man Tamang, a former forestry employee of His Majesty's Government, he surveyed Nepal's tiger reserves.

They selected as a prime area for study Royal Chitwan National Park, located in the lowland south, a region called *terai*, near the Indian border. Chitwan had numerous advantages: it was near Kathmandu, it already had housing facilities and elephants for transportation and a tiger population that was well known thanks to a commercial tourist operation called Tiger Tops Jungle Lodge. In its ungulate biomass, Chitwan was unique on the Asian subcontinent. The only megafauna to have gone extinct recently were wild elephants, swamp deer, and wild water buffalo.

Wildlife management and biology did not mix well at the time. A classic conflict over the management of grizzlies and mountain lions had just erupted in the United States, a clash Seidensticker was well aware of from his work with mountain lions. The Smithsonian proposal thus focused only on scientific investigation, leaving the technical and socioeconomic matters of conservation to international and Nepali agencies. Yet the international agencies, just like the Indian government, remained cool to the idea of scientific investigation as a tool for conservationists. The Food and Agricultural Organization of the United Nations Development Program representative in Kathmandu and the World Wildlife Fund International in 1973 were proposing their own plan to the Nepal government and saw the Smithsonian

Facing extinction in the wild, the magnificent Bengal tiger powerfully symbolizes the need for scientific research to support efforts to save endangered species.

Rivers from the midlands and snow peaks of the Himalayas converge in the lowlands of Nepal's Royal Chitwan National Park. Along the rivers lie extensive stands of tall grass, virtually all that remains of this once-widespread South Asian habitat. Tigers, leopards, sloth bears, four species of deer, and some of the world's last remaining greater one-horned rhinos live in the park, where tall grass may camouflage even a two-ton rhino from a person on foot. For nearly two decades, scientists working in Chitwan have tracked tigers on elephant back, long enough to follow some tigers from birth to death. Tiger Tops, a tourist lodge, provides field biologists with a base at the western edge of the park.

suggestion as competitive. They felt that limited funds should be spent immediately on practical conservation measures. But then, rather dramatically, the U.S. National Appeal of the World Wildlife Fund decided to ignore the parent organization's advice and announced that it would fund the Smithsonian project with $160,000 over three years. This caused a considerable amount of grumbling in international conservation circles, but the Smithsonian went ahead and signed an agreement with His Majesty's Government in late 1973 calling for two principle investigators—one from each nation—and specifying protocols. It had taken nearly five years to sell the Tiger Ecology Project and the difficulties were just beginning.

Things got off to a promising start scientifically. "The first 25 days were a great success," wrote John Seidensticker at the time. "We darted a tiger, but the drug did not inject. Got her again later. She has a transmitter on and it is working fine." But in other areas things were awry. There were administrative delays in funding, thus worrying His Majesty's Government, and transportation requirements had been underestimated: the scientists had no vehicles of their own, and there weren't enough elephants for them to use. In the tall grasses (up to twenty-five feet) of the park, inhabited by large and dangerous animals like sloth bears and rhinos, elephants were virtually the only way to get around. Moreover, the people at Tiger Tops, on the west end of the park, were aghast at the thought of their tourist clientele coming to Nepal to see wild tigers and seeing instead oversized kitties with gaily colored collars around their necks. Some observers declared the project to be a failure, but the Smithsonian persevered. The administrative matters were gradually resolved, the Smithsonian purchased more elephants, and the researchers agreed only to collar tigers that were found west of a central guard station.

As Melvin Sunquist, who followed Seidensticker as coprincipal in-

Like most other cats, tigers are secretive creatures of shadowy forests. Tigers rely on stealth to stalk their prey, approaching silently to within a few feet of an unsuspecting axis deer or sambar before lunging to deliver a killing neck bite. The killed prey is then dragged into thick cover where the tiger feeds intermittently until the carcass is consumed, usually within a day or so. Tigers may go five to seven days between successful hunts. Creatures of the plains, cheetahs display different hunting strategies. Cheetahs chase and finally outrun their prey, which they knock down with a forepaw blow before delivering the killing neck bite. Cheetahs do not stay with kills very long and frequently lose them to larger predators such as lions, leopards, and hyenas.

vestigator in 1974, has written: "Any short-term study of a long-lived animal is only a glimpse." The Tiger Ecology Project proved to be not only a long-lived but also a multispecies investigation of virtually all aspects of the tiger's natural habitat.

Tigers are cryptic cats. They live alone, usually in dense cover. They depend on stealth to catch their prey: except for cheetahs, no big cats can endure an extended chase. It would take a long time to collect much information on these beasts, such as how large their home range is, how they use the resources it provides—for example, what they prey on—and how these solitary animals communicate with one another.

Troubles continued to plague the project. In February 1976 Sunquist and Tamang darted a big male east of the boundary. It had the number 02 tattooed on its ear, identifying it as a tiger that had lost its collar shortly after being captured by Seidensticker two years earlier. Sunquist showed a polaroid of the tiger to Chuck McDougal, the director of wildlife at Tiger Tops, and he immediately recognized it as "the Dakre tiger," one that frequented the buffalo bait at Tiger Tops. The result for science was the insight that the Dakre tiger used a far larger range than anyone had believed: the diplomatic result of a Tiger Tops tiger wearing a collar was a sudden deterioration in relations. Shikaris from both camps exchanged bodily threats from elephant back when they chanced to meet on opposite sides of a stream. His Majesty's Government intervened, declaring that any tiger in the park was fair game for the scientists. Subsequently, relations improved. McDougal now cooperates with the National Zoo in recording his own careful observations of the tigers.

Shortly after the Dakre tiger was darted, Tamang was attacked by a female tiger while he was trying to climb a tree. The tiger climbed up after him. His leg was so badly torn that he was incapacitated for nine months. Then another tiger died during immobilization and His Majesty's Government barred further tiger captures until, a month later, the researchers were able to show that the animal had been weakened by extensive infections from previous injuries of unknown origin.

Meanwhile, a picture of the overall ecosystem of Chitwan was emerging. An early question concerned leopards. Generally, where tigers are in abundance, there aren't many leopards. This is called interspecific social dominance, which is to say that the much larger tiger will attack leopards and drive them away. Over the first few years of the Tiger Ecology Project, careful attention to leopard kills and collaring of the animals shed light on how the two big cats coexist at Chitwan.

To begin with, the tiger preys on larger species of the many ungulates in the park—sambar and axis deer and the like—while the leopard preys on smaller species like hog deer and barking deer. In addition, leopards seem to keep a close eye on where the tigers are: for example, in the riverine forest, tall grass habitat of Chitwan, officials and locals annually will burn part of the forest to promote the growth of grass that is used for thatching roofs. The fire, and the resulting lack of dense cover, drives the larger deer into the forest and the tiger hunts there. The leopard leaves the forest and preys among

the burnt stalks. As soon as the new grass provides cover, the tiger returns and the leopard heads for the forest. Tigers will use roads to travel on; leopards keep to other pathways.

Both animals were believed to be nocturnal, or crepuscular, and thus inactive during the daylight hours, but researchers found that both do move around during the day, presumably hunting. The tigers are less likely to be active during especially hot days and evenings, reserving the cool early morning for their hunts. The leopards are frequently active during the day and early evening. In short, the subordinate leopard must be more flexible to survive in the same area as the dominant tiger. In Chitwan, the coexistence is aided by an unusually rich ungulate fauna—there is a higher biomass (combined weight) of prey species than in other areas, and a large proportion of it is made up of smaller species, like hog deer. Also, there is a lot of dense cover making it easier for the leopards to avoid the tigers.

Tigers, it was found after several years of observation and daily eavesdropping on radio transmissions, were extremely mobile, traveling up to twenty kilometers in a given night. Much of this behavior is hunting, but not all. Tigers spend a fair portion of their time patrolling the upland or sal forest where their prey is scarce. What are they doing there? Evidently maintaining their exclusive ranges. They are strictly territorial. Each female has her own territory and it overlaps with no other female's territory. Males have exclusive territories as well, but a male's territory may overlap several female territories. Young tigers eventually have to leave the area: territories change hands only upon the death of a prior occupant. The death of a male opens up that territory only to another male; the same is true for female territories.

Young tigers may remain in their mother's range for two years or longer, well after they are independent, especially if food is abundant. Sunquist points out that this gives the young access to important information—hunting techniques and criteria for suitable home ranges and den sites. This is the last true sociability the tiger experiences except for sexual encounters; several tigers may associate at one kill in times of exceptional food abundance, but this is very rarely observed. For the remainder of their lives the young tigers will patrol their range, hunting and marking its borders with urine, feces, and scrapes, places where the tiger scrapes away a small amount of vegetation.

This relatively rigid, tradition-bound lifestyle survives in an ecosystem that itself is in constant flux. The seasons, the flooding of the rivers, even changes in the river's course all make subtle and not-so-subtle alterations in the vegetation. Naturally, the burning has profound effects each year too. Underlying the "grid" of tiger territories, the land is changing at all times. New grass brings certain of the ungulates into an area: later when the grass has grown high, others move in, such as hog deer. As the cover grows yet more dense and tangled along the edges of forest, sambar lurk in nearly perfect hiding. And with each such change, so too must there be change in the activities of the predators. Chitwan's nature as a complex and dynamic park was emerging.

Principal investigators came and went, their particular projects

(Following pages) That tigers such as these still live in the wild is in part due to the efforts of National Zoo scientists.

180

The use of safe and effective immobilizing drugs together with radio telemetry, both techniques pioneered by John Seidensticker (pictured left) and other National Zoo scientists, is the only way to study large dangerous mammals living in densely vegetated habitats. Using these techniques in Nepal, zoo scientists gathered information on tigers, leopards, and other species that has been essential to the management of the park. The development of radio transmitters powered by lithium batteries means that a tiger need be immobilized only once every three to five years for scientists to follow it throughout its life.

complete. Tamang was followed by Hemanta Mishra, who carried out detailed studies of the ungulate population. Sunquist's work was continued by James L. David Smith, who concentrated on the dispersal of tigers and gathered some of the most detailed information on a large carnivore ever to be documented. Meanwhile, it became clear that if more tigers than the fifteen adults present in the park were to achieve protection, more land was needed—since the tiger is so rigidly stingy about its own territory. In 1980, His Majesty King Birendra Bir Bikram Shah Deva enacted a law establishing the King Mahendra Nature Conservation Trust as a nongovernmental organization enabled to raise the funds for wildlife conservation and activities in Nepal. This allows Nepal to continue its conservation activities free of outside technical assistance and to this degree the Smithsonian program has succeeded precisely as had been hoped: a large number of Nepalis have been trained in the techniques of wildlife research and conservation and have developed supportive peer relationships with U.S. scientists; a great deal of crucial scientific information has been generated; and the entire idea of conservation has become institutionalized in Nepal. Based on the information about tigers garnered from the project, Seidensticker was able to investigate the tiger populations of Java, Sumatra, and Bangladesh and on behalf of the World Wildlife Fund make well-thought out and practical recommendations to those countries for their own tiger conservation projects. Good science, it has been shown, coupled with perseverance and respect, can be the bedrock of true conservation.

As the Nepal project continued, it focused chiefly on the other spectacular and endangered animal at Chitwan, the greater one-horned Asian rhinoceros, the largest of the ungulate population and in some ways, the most important. The rhino is a sacred animal in Nepal's religion and it is integral to ceremonial life. Part of the land that became Royal Chitwan National Park had previously been designated a rhino reserve when the region began to be developed for agriculture in the 1960s: without the rhinos there most likely would not have been a Chitwan Park. Researchers are finding that rhinos are one of the

181

most important features of—even causes of—the ecological dynamism of Chitwan.

In 1983 tropical ecologist Eric Dinerstein became the fourth American coprincipal investigator for the project. His mission was to follow rhinos over twenty-four-hour periods to document how much time they spend "grazing, browsing, wallowing, resting, walking, musing, and politicking." A great deal of the time, evidently, rhinos don't do much at all, making the biologist's task tedious in some ways. But there are compensations. As Dinerstein wrote to Wemmer at Front Royal, who has since 1977 been the coordinating uncle of the Nepal project: "During the monsoon, the elephant grasses leap 25 feet into the air. Lianas and creepers probe the secrets of the forest canopy with their tendrils. We no longer enter the jungle; rather it swallows

Greater one-horned rhinoceros are a major component of Chitwan's fauna. Twenty years ago, much of the valley was severely overgrazed as rhinos and domestic cattle competed for food. Today cattle are no longer permitted to graze in the park, an important step in securing the future of the rhinos.

us whole. More than ever, let us now praise famous elephants. Without these noble creatures, we would flail miserably through an impenetrable labyrinth of vegetation. They provide us safe passage. . . . Sitting on an elephant and observing rhinos at the edge of a tall grass patch, the rhinos seem dwarfed by the wall of green. Yet these same animals are over 4 meters long from snout to stern and weigh nearly two tons. . . . Being aboard an elephant while following rhinos must be the closest one can come on terra firma to whale watching. The buck and sway of the elephant as it rolls through the sea of tall grass feels like the heaving of a ship in hot pursuit of a pod of cetaceans. The analogy is not too far-fetched: during the monsoon the rough beasts we study slouch towards their forest walls or submerge their ballast in a river. In an attempt to cool their prodigious heels, rhinos became semi-aquatic."

For the male rhinos, life involves a great deal of warfare. One male will gain hegemony over a group of females for a time, only to be bested by another male in battles that inflict many wounds, often serious, and occasionally fatal. This is hard on the animals individually, but good for genetic diversity within the herd for even when the population is small, no male's genes will dominate. As Dinerstein points out, "Careful study of individual rhinoceros permits insights into the breeding biology of this endangered species that are as important to conservation as the construction of any guard post or jungle track."

The rhino is beginning to be seen as a horticulturalist with continuing effects on the forest itself. During the winter the rhinos spend a lot of their time browsing on the leaves and twigs of kutmiro, a common tree of the avocado family. This pruning, or a kind of "bonsai horticulture," evidently has a major influence on forest structure, since without it the widespread kutmiro tree would rapidly grow up to the canopy and perhaps begin to crowd out the canopy species now present. Dinerstein has recently completed his study of the rhino and is now analyzing the final results.

A major study under way is on another forest "management" effect of the rhinos. A favored rhino food is a fruit called trewia. The seeds, ingested by the rhinos, are deposited in their dung in what appear to be special latrine areas—some in the forest and some in the grasslands. Those that are deposited in grassland areas tend to grow fast and well; those in forests do not do as well. By this regular activity, the rhinos aid the forest in colonizing the grasslands.

In Kathmandu, one can see temples where in the courtyard the secular business of winnowing rice goes on regularly. In Chitwan, a preserve for animals and a unique ecosystem, thousands of people arrive each year to harvest the tall grasses for thatch. Human intervention, in the form of controlled burning, is an important part of the system, as is the intervention of the rhinos. Recalling his time at Chitwan and the results that have emerged from the Nepal project, Seidensticker pointed out that Chitwan shows us an entirely different way to think about a park or reserve as a natural resource for people and animals, somehow akin to the religious and secular use of a temple. As Seidensticker says: "We need to think of these reserves around the world as sacred groves."

People and wildlife coexist in the Chitwan Valley, in the shadow of the highest peaks of the Himalayas (next page) just eighty miles away, thus preserving its natural beauty for Nepal and the rest of the world.

COMMITMENT

Above the canopy of broad green leaves it is humid. Below the canopy it is more so. Water condenses from the saturated tropical atmosphere, and the droplets wiggle-waggle down the veins of the waxy leaves, dripping from their decurved tips onto other leaves and into the tangled root masses of bromeliads, plants eking out a living high in the treetops, sustained not by the earth but by bark and air and passing chance.

Cebus monkeys ply hairy, ropelike lianas that loop down from on high. Butterflies flutter and float beneath the canopy. Vines cling to tree trunks. Water drips. Chaste waxy orchids—lavender, white, yellow, pink—peek out from the proletariat of ferns, each flower carefully labeled.

This is a tropical rain forest. This particular one doesn't exist yet, except in architects' plans and in the dreams of Michael Robinson, the director of the National Zoo. With any luck it will rise up enclosed in a great dome where the polar bears once lived. (They have been moved to a cooler climate.) Thanks to the terrain of that area in the zoo, visitors will be able to ascend the hill and look in on life in the canopy of the forest, something that has taken wildlife biologists years of ingenuity to accomplish in the wild. Observers will see jaguars and tapirs roaming the forest floor, separated by invisible clear plastic barriers. Below, from yet another vantage point, one will be able to press one's nose against a glass window and see the aquatic life of a tropical stream swim by, varieties of fish and their predators, such as otters, the two factions again separated but seen together.

The tropical rain forest is the most complex ecosystem known. The attempt by the zoo will be to create a fragment of such a forest, real and alive. Impossible? A few miles from the zoo, there is a functioning

coral reef—it is an ecosystem that works with a minimum of outside input—lights, a wavemaking device, and the occasional injection of food items. It was built by Walter Adey, and thousands upon thousands of visitors to the Smithsonian's National Museum of Natural History can watch it work, getting as close to a coral reef as no doubt many of them ever will. And because it is so accessible it has become a valuable research arena, just as zoo collections have so frequently provided insights unattainable from the wild.

The very process of producing a tropical forest in the valley of Rock Creek will no doubt produce biological insights of many sorts. The Smithsonian milieu is ideal: with the zoo staff and the curators at the National Museum of Natural History and the people at the Smithsonian Tropical Research Institute on Barro Colorado in Panama, the Institution is the greatest single repository of biological knowledge of the tropics anywhere.

Why go to the bother and the financial effort? The answer goes to the heart of Robinson's goals for the zoo.

People generally love animals. This is attested to by the millions of people who keep pets—for all sorts of complex reasons, perhaps, but not out of necessity. It is witnessed to also by the half million or so members of humane societies, the hundreds of thousands of people who subscribe to wildlife magazines, and locally by the three million people a year who enter the gates of the National Zoo. Many of the most beautiful and interesting animals they see are tropical in origin, and many of those are endangered. The zoo's captive breeding programs play an urgent role in preserving biological diversity and are rescuing from extinction at least some of nature's masterpieces. Their success is ultimately failure, however, if a species saved in captivity has no hope of returning to the wild. Habitat is crucial, and it is vanishing at an alarming rate, especially in tropical countries, virtually all of which exist in the Third World. It is vanishing in the tropics not out of ignorance, but out of greed, in some cases, and mostly need, or in other words, poverty.

What role, then, does a temperate-zone zoo—or for that matter, a temperate-zone country—have?

It is difficult to be concerned about the fate of an animal you have never seen. Even a two-dimensional film representation of an animal does not have anywhere near the same effect as seeing one in the flesh, hearing it, smelling it. The usual response to such a real-life sight—whether in a zoo or in the wild—is emotional or, as Robinson says, irrational. It is possible, he believes, to convert this irrational response into rational action. Surveys of zoogoers show that they are mostly well-educated adults, just the sort of people who could be inspired to become doers.

Robinson is aware also that it is pretty hard to get concerned about rain forests if you don't know what one is. He would like to have people experience a bit of rain forest with all of their senses, to build an emotional bridge between Rock Creek and the tropics.

The zoo, then, will become even more intensely a great big conservation message, a consciousness-raising park. Wherever possible, the message will be to conserve habitat. Part of the zoo's master plan is to

Along with diverse animals, other wonders of the tropical rain forest—from lush, tree-blanketed precipices to exquisite Cattleya David Sweet orchids—will be displayed under the dome of the National Zoo's planned Amazonia exhibit. Zoo visitors will thus learn to appreciate the intricate relationships between all living things—relationships that achieve their greatest complexity in the rain forest. Techniques pioneered in developing coral reef exhibits will help the zoo to recreate a slice of rain forest in the center of Washington.

attempt, as other zoos have, to produce an African veldt habitat where there is now a parking lot. There, herbivores and carnivores will roam more freely in an area closer to their native ecological context. Habitats are, of course, chiefly vegetative, and Robinson sees the zoo as becoming in effect a biopark. He plans all kinds of new plantings to celebrate the variety of floral life. The butterfly garden and a proud stand of sunflowers are harbingers of the kind of exhibits that will focus on animal and plant interactions. Already an enormous wire net enclosure surrounded by branches and trees and equipped with rope ladders and swings allows gibbons—the most acrobatic of all the apes—to play naturally and entertainingly on Gibbon Ridge. In front of the Bird House, ducks, geese, herons, and other waterfowl enjoy a miniature marsh habitat known as the Wetlands Exhibit. Aquatic exhibits are also in store for the future.

The goal in all this is to foster an understanding of ecosystems. As Robinson has written: "Scientists and animal lovers would be an ideal constituency for a pressure group on tropical deforestation. . . . The rain forest has the potential to be the focus of a scientific crusade. . . . At the outset a campaign to save the rain forests would need to have a program for research and a program for conservation." These things will have to come in some large part from nations such as the United States. The scientific resources of the Third World are simply not at present adequate to undertake such a task. On the conservation side, one of Robinson's former colleagues at Barro Colorado, Ira Rubinoff, has put forth an imaginative plan. He proposes a levy, similar to that of OPEC, on the wealthy nations—based on their population and GNP—to create a fund to subsidize nations that preserve their forests. This would provide a cash alternative to nations in desperate need.

"I would argue," Robinson says, "that no major exhibit should lack a conservation message. No technique of interactive graphics should be ignored in getting across the message. The ultimate connection between animals and habitats has to be made. . . . You can't save the giant panda without saving the bamboo." The National Zoo intends to develop a constituency of activists from the throngs of zoogoers. Such people, properly motivated, could be a powerful influence on elected officials with responsibilities for tropical research budgets.

The research at the zoo will go on, increasingly cooperative with museums, universities and government laboratories, increasingly interdisciplinary, and, even as applied science proliferates, increasingly fundamental. As Robert McC. Adams, secretary of the Smithsonian, said of the zoo's future: "Research is engraved on that place in the foreseeable future—broad ecological focus, behavioral studies, and all the science arising from the care of the collection. The zoo represents a major human and capital investment and what they are doing is altogether consistent with the philosophy and the mandate of the Smithsonian, the increase and diffusion of knowledge."

The National Zoo is the only zoo in the country that is funded chiefly by the federal government. FONZ provides a percentage of the annual operating budget and is an important supporter of zoo research—both with funds and volunteers—but the zoo depends primar-

The Zoo is now highlighting the more than ninety-nine percent of animal species that are not land-living vertebrates—the countless fish, aquatic invertebrates, and insects that comprise most of the world's biological diversity.

ily on federal money. That is to say, it is the zoo of all our citizens. And as these citizens visit the zoo, they can take pride that behind the scenes is a remarkable group of scientists caring not only for the animals in the collections but for the future of wildlife around the globe. Zoogoers can also take satisfaction in the distant Conservation and Research Center in Front Royal, Virginia. There, Christen Wemmer hopes to redouble the efforts in conservation biology and add new Species Survival Plan animals.

"Wildlife reserves around the world are becoming more and more like zoos," he says. "They are both islands, in a sense, and the animals within them have to be managed in similar ways. For example, Chitwan is a long narrow place with two male tigers. The two could begin to be too dominant in the gene pool at Chitwan. How do you manage that? We don't know yet. A few years back one male tiger, number 105, died and while transient males sorted things out, there were three years of social upheaval among the tigers. These are the kinds of things we have to learn how to do."

Wemmer hopes that more biologists from the Third World will join in the wildlife management training program operated by Rudy Rudran. "We have to help these nations create their own conservation infrastructure," he explains.

Thus, the National Zoo is not only all of ours, but an international zoo as well. It is one of the best hopes for the world's animals.

We read a lot these days in the newspapers about institutions that grew up around some wonderful idea or some dramatically necessary invention only to lose sight of the original fiery idea and diversify into other realms, becoming bureaucratic, ossified, remote. This cannot happen at the National Zoo, for it and other similar institutions have a built-in corrective mechanism. Every day the zoo must account for the compelling needs of the animals in its care. They need food, attention, space, and understanding. For many, survival depends as well on records of their faring as individuals and species. No one I have met who remains for long in the zoo's employ ever forgets this, or is driven by anything less than a desire to do this better each day.

As I write these last words, I hear on a television set in the other room that a soft-drink company has paid $470 million to acquire another soft-drink company, the better to control the market. Readers of this book may recognize the possible origins of such territoriality; they may also share my amazement at the thought that the cost of that soda pop company is eleven times the entire annual expenditure in this country for tropical biological research. Perhaps there is no point in making invidious comparisons between soda pop and the miracle of life's diversity.

Just come to the zoo. It offers both.

The giant panda, so gravely endangered in the wild and so greatly admired by people around the world, continues to symbolize the National Zoo's commitment to giving people the opportunity to see such marvelous exotic creatures while working to save them so that future generations may have the same opportunity.

AFTERWORD

The Once and Future Zoo

The National Zoo was established in 1889 and in the hundred years since its founding, Washington, D.C., the United States, and the world have all changed beyond recognition. The city has crept outward so that the zoo's site, once in unspoiled countryside, is now well within the perimeters of urban sprawl. The Smithsonian Institution, our parent organization, has almost fully occupied the Mall, now encompassing the world's largest concatenation of galleries, museums, and research entities. Since 1889 the James Smithson bequest for "the increase and diffusion of knowledge" has resulted in the creation of museums devoted to natural history, American history, air and space technology, African art, American art, and many other subjects.

The world has witnessed many profound changes in the last hundred years. There has been an immense improvement in the condition of humankind, in food, shelter, health, education, and culture. With this have come alterations in our attitudes about human welfare and that of other species. Political freedom has extended in parallel with democracy, empires have come and gone, there have been two immensely destructive world wars and dozens of smaller ones. What other species has ever killed millions of individuals in conflict rather than predation?

The development of harnessed nuclear power is the climax of a series of inventions that enormously increased our power and mobility. Fusion power stands on the threshold for tomorrow. But there are changes that I think are more significant than immeasurably increased mechanical power. Certainly the most substantial, even epochal, of these is the present environmental impact of our species. Humankind has reached the stage of being numerous beyond the projection of our forebears one hundred years ago. Partly as a consequence of our burgeoning billions we are now a *terrapernicious* force, menacing the diversity of life on earth. Where once we struggled against nature in order to survive, now we menace the existence of much of nature. We are destroying the rain forests in a manner comparable to that of one of the vast geological cataclysms of past ages. Species are falling at an increasing rate as our population explodes and our economic development surges ahead. Our destruction of forests and consumption of fossilized remains of past life have produced a major threat to the stability of our global climate. The greenhouse effect is with us, and sober scientists are proposing some cures for overheating that are staggering in their scope. For instance, it has been calculated that planting 720,000 square miles of new forest would remove about one billion tons of carbon dioxide annually—a third of the problem! This is afforestation on an unprecedented scale. Another suggestion is that we should load the stratosphere with sulphur dioxide gas to reflect the heat. Why not instead correct our environmental sins at ground level by applying some holistic biology?

All this has happened when science has extended our knowledge and control at an unprecedented rate and to an unpredicted extent. My own choice for the single most revolutionary discovery of the last one hundred years—revolutionary in its potentially still unrealized effect on history—is the discovery of the genetic code by James Watson and Francis Crick. This discovery unlocked the ultimate secret of life on earth. All these factors together frame the context of scientific and technological progress, alongside environmental stupidity, in which we must view the next one hundred years. What will the zoo's second century bring?

The Future?

The future of zoos is intimately connected with the global environmental crisis because it profoundly affects their role. In particular, it gives both emphasis and vital urgency to their educational function. The public at large, and decision makers in particular, must understand the interconnectedness of the living world, our role in the pattern of life on earth, and the nature of our involuntary but real stewardship of the planet Earth. This role for zoos has already been accentuated by the galloping urbanization of our society, prior to our global crisis. The environmental crisis gives it extreme and desperate urgency. The new millennium, just around the corner, will need biologically sophisticated citizens if its promise is not to be lost. In the Middle Ages, the hallmark of an educated and cultivated person was knowledge of Latin and Greek and training in theology. In the twenty-first century, a knowledge of biology will certainly occupy a similar central place. All the major problems that we face in the immediate and near future are centered on the effects of our biology on our lives and those of other living things. Even if we solve the crises of environmental destruction and diminishing biodiversity, other

significant biologically based problems would still exist. For instance, although genetic engineering has great potential for transforming nature in a revolutionary way, it would need broad education to be put in perspective and to be used wisely. Because of all this, we are proposing to transform our zoological park into a biological park. What this entails is relatively simple in concept. The history of the development of the idea is also worth telling.

BioParks: General Theory and Principles

The BioPark would combine elements of existing zoos, aquariums, natural history museums, botanic gardens, arboretums, and ethnological/anthropological museums to create a holistic form of bioexhibitry. Essentially a bioexhibit should portray life in all its interconnectedness. Creating the BioPark means ending a series of unnatural separations. It means exhibiting plants and animals, not plants *or* animals (as in botanic gardens and zoos). It also means that aquatic organisms belong in the same exhibition complex as terrestrial ones. Exhibits about the structure, functional interpretation, and history of life on earth belong inseparably with exhibits of living plants and animals. At present these elements of biology and paleontology are housed separately in museums, zoos, aquariums and botanic gardens. Inextricably interacting in the real world, they are institutionally riven apart by our culture. This disjunction of a unified subject makes cross-referencing and holistic education extraordinarily difficult to achieve. It is regrettable that we so arrange our public institutions that one can only see the skeleton of an elephant at a great distance from the place where one can see the live animal. We say,

in effect, look at the elephant's skull and then catch the bus to the zoo and look at an elephant's head!

We also separate the history of our species (including our paleontology and prehistory) from the rest of the animal kingdom. Not only are we part of the pattern of life on earth, an evolutionary product like every other organism, but we have for several thousand years profoundly affected the world's biota. The BioPark is a place to tell this story of our evolution, ancestry, and the growth of human culture, art, and artifacts. It is also, perhaps even more urgently, a place to document, describe, and illustrate our effect on the living planet and its future. This means that *Australopithecus*, the paintings of Lascaux cave, Egyptian hieroglyphics, and the greenhouse effect all belong somewhere in the BioPark.

Most of the institutions that would contribute to the BioPark have highly important functions that are separable from their public education and recreation role. Museums are repositories for the archives of history, whether this be the history of science and technology, art, society, or politics. They are also centers of research based on objects. Of course, we cannot and must not substitute for the separate archival and research functions of museums. Such functions could not conceivably be dealt with in the space available to the BioPark. So there is a very considerable practical and utilitarian separation between public exhibit objects and research collections. This separation is now recognized, in practice, by the establishment of museum support centers, housing objects for research and storage away from the expensive downtown areas where museums often are located. Most existing zoos are an exception to the generalization about the exhibit collection being distinct from the research collection. Their collections are largely limited to exhibits and can be immensely valuable assets for research.

Clearly the full interpretation of the world of life on earth, envisaged for the BioPark, is best achieved through the collaboration of the entities from which it will draw. The National Zoological Park's membership in the Smithsonian family puts it in a rare position to develop a holistic multidisciplinary approach. There are experts on almost everything at the Smithsonian; it is unique in the world of exhibitry in its diversity and its unity of management. A similar concentration of expertise is not generally assembled in one area, but there are obvious possibilities elsewhere. For example, New York's Central Park Zoo faces the American Museum of Natural History. What an opportunity for joint programs and cross-referencing!

What keeps institutions apart is partly the ossifying effects of their separate histories and the "dynamics" of institutional evolution. Often the park department runs the zoo, the education department runs the discovery center, and a board of trustees runs the city museum. Committeedom militates against holism and networking. This is reflected in our education system where universities have become subdivided into fiefdoms that separate where they should unite.

When I was an undergraduate, many years ago, I came across an article by the plant geneticist C. D. Darlington arguing for the unification of biology in the universities. I have just remembered this marvelous polemic and rediscovered it. Most of his proposals remain dead letters. But his observations cry out for emphasis now. They are just as applicable to bioexhibits as to academic seats of learning. Darlington (1962,74) argues that the fragmentation of biology has resulted "in the reduction of botany and zoology to ritual introduction to medicine, and in the general use of the term 'biology' to where it has no meaning, indeed to cover up the absence of biology, *the failure to connect plants, animals, and Man*" (my emphasis). Furthermore, Darlington outlines the benefits of holism (1962,74): "The consequences of beginning to teach biology, real and unified biology, would be far-reaching. The smallest consequence would be that the word biology would be somewhat less used than it is today, for it would acquire a genuine meaning instead of a sham meaning. A middling consequence would concern medicine and the social sciences. They would acquire what at present they lack, a theoretical frame and foundation, a coherence with science as a whole. But the largest and slowest consequence would be very great indeed. It would mean that ordinary education would find itself in a position to provide ordinary people with an understanding of what happens to them in life: an understanding of their place in the scheme of things. Such an understanding would lead to a revolution in human affairs in the next hundred years as profound as that arising from the development of the physical sciences in the last hundred years." All this was said more than twenty-five years ago, before we realized the depth of our environmental crisis. I do not share Darlington's optimistic conviction that an understanding of holistic biology "would" change the world, but I do feel that without it there is no hope.

Origins

We have progressed a long way from the penitentiary-like zoos of the past that were founded on the principle of a gallery of exotic and bizarre animals. Zoos had their origins as royal menageries, symbols of pomp, but they have outlived their disgraceful beginnings as have so many of our institutions. More than four thousand years ago the Chinese had a large zoo, called a Garden of Intelligence, and the Egyptians assembled a large number of animals at Saqqara. Down through the ages, menageries distinguished the royal courts; they were "cabinets of curiosities." At court, and in fashionable houses of the aristocracy, monkeys were exhibited in sumptuous clothes and cheetahs had jeweled collars, just as today film stars are seen with exotic pets.

Botanic gardens have almost as long a history as zoos. Plants were collected and propagated for their utility in medicine and agriculture and for their beauty. Research into herbal medicine, even at the dawn of history, gave gardens a much more respectable parentage than zoos, and they have continued to maintain this distinctive legitimacy. Today the spectacle function of botanic gardens continues to be secondary to research and propagation. In fact the earliest gardens functioned much more as centers of propagation than zoos ever did, or do even now. The spectacle function of zoos militated against much breeding, as did the difficulty of acquiring and pairing breeding collections of most animal species. In general, and without underestimating the skills of gardeners, it is easier to provide satisfactory growing conditions for exotic plants than it is to rear and breed exotic animals. Furthermore, it is easier to propagate most plants by layering, grafting, budding, making cuttings, and producing and planting seeds than it is to maintain exotic animals in breeding condition. Of course most of the plants raised in botanic gardens are not the botanical equivalent of elephants, rhinos, and giraffes. Breeding a kapok tree in Boston may be the logistic equivalent of breeding an elephant in Washington, D.C.

Having said this it is possible to identify the historical reasons for the continuous and continued separation of plants and animals in zoos and botanic gardens. Aquariums, public exhibits of aquatic creatures, really date to the ready availability of glass. Before that, captive aquatic animals were kept in ornamental ponds, particularly in China and Japan, but they could not produce a true spectacle when viewed from above alone. (It is worth noting that the selective breeding of carp, in the Orient, produced animals that were conspicuously colored from above—as in goldfish and koi. Fishes that are brightly colored in nature are adapted to the function of communication within the water, not to signal to terrestrial animals above it.) Aquariums tended to be located originally at the seaside or close to the sea because of the greater richness of marine fishes that needed access to a good supply of seawater for their maintenance. Early aquariums were at Rostock, Monte Carlo, Plymouth, and similar port cities. Only in the twentieth century, when transportation improved so dramatically, did the jewel-like fishes of tropical freshwaters become available to temperate region peoples. There are now hundreds of millions of "pet" fishes imported into the United States. Aquariums, as spectacles, can be truly marvelous because of color, shapes, and continual movement. Few zoo exhibits can ever be as active as a tankful of different fishes. Aquariums can also be packed into relatively small chunks

of real estate; they seldom have the space to include terrestrial collections. They are perhaps, therefore, separatists by virtue of economics as well as philosophy.

The natural history museums of the world, now virtually universal, originated in the capital cities of mercantile powers (often the administrative centers of empires) as repositories of the spoils of exploration and trade. Curiosities of nature that could not be brought back alive for menageries or gardens were brought back as skins, to be stuffed and mounted, or as skeletons, dried specimens, or nonperishable hardparts. Later fossils were added to the collections. Such museums were located in contact with universities, medical academies, or academies of science and often had a major involvement in descriptive, classificatory research. Cataloging the collection, as in a fine arts museum, led to classifying the world of life. Because they were/are building-bound, museums seldom had the space for living materials, even when the problems of husbandry were solved. Twenty bear skeletons, a thousand bird skins, and hundreds of thousands of insect specimens can be stored in the space needed to keep two living Asian elephants! Even now, when some museums progressively add live specimens, these are usually restricted to insects or aquatic animals in the aquariums.

New Exhibits: Predictions, Far In to Far Out

What will the BioPark look like? What will we see at the National Zoo in 1990, 2000, and 2089? In the short term the predictions are relatively easy. The trends are already established. We will have commenced construction of a holistic BioPark exhibit, Amazonia, by 1990. When completed it will unite the

world of plants and animals, terrestrial and aquatic, into one exhibit. It will highlight tropical biology as a science in which the Smithsonian has high expertise and focus on the problems of equating economic development with the sustenance of biodiversity. It will emphasize the detailed interactivity and interconnectedness of tropical ecosystems and be a tribute to the extraordinary fine-tuning achieved by the evolutionary process in its most dramatic and intense expression. Fishes in profusion will swim actively, weaving patterns of color; other aquatic animals will fascinate, and the river will be set in a tropical forest of Breughelian intricacy. Allusions to the never-absent Amerindian human influence will be made in the exhibit, and the associated Gallery of Tropical Life will focus on teeming complexity. Sooner or later, and sooner I hope, we will begin to create exhibits that reflect the animal's perceptions of the world as well as our own. In the area of visual perceptions alone this is important and extraordinarily fertile ground. People at large need to know that very few animals see the world as we see it. This is known to most organismic biologists and has been an early emphasis of classical ethology, but it is largely undisseminated knowledge. Anthropomorphisms about animals abound and we reinforce them by presenting, in zoos, a human-eye picture of habitats. We "paint" them in our colors, build them to our scale, and focus them to our viewpoint. It is only when we "see" dogs detecting scents that we can never smell, or cats hearing sounds "invisible" to our ears, that we commonly have any inkling of the differences in animal perceptions.

Elsewhere in the growing BioPark there will be an increasing emphasis on plant/animal interactions. These will include a Pollination Hall, appropriately associated with the Invertebrate Exhibit, that will show the complexity and wonder of the world of flowers that largely, but not entirely, evolved in response to the perceptual worlds of their predominantly insect pollinators. Butterflies, bees, hummingbirds, and bats will provide a colorful moving tableau in which a profusion of flowering plants will be set. Models of flowers will illustrate complex floral mechanisms, and large models will permit small people to explore flowers as if they were bees, butterflies, or moths. We will also illustrate the visual world of insects by giving bee's eye views of a technicolor that differs markedly from our own. Skeletons of extinct ancestors of elephants will enhance the newly refurbished large mammal house, and the rhino yard will show how these animals profoundly affect the plant communities within their range. By the year 2000 technology now in its infancy will be used to illustrate structure and function. Perhaps computer-enhanced tomography will be used to display the inner structures of some large animals, and large screen displays of satellite-derived imagery will highlight the world distribution of weather, human populations, and ecosystems. Science galleries will show progress in biology, medicine, and life-related sciences. Art will appear alongside the animals and plants that inspired it, and we may have recreated some of the paleolithic cave paintings from Europe. Endangered species breeding and reintroduction programs will be supplemented by ever-increasing emphasis on the cryopreservation of life propagules and highly developed techniques derived from studies of reproductive biology. The National BioPark will be a friendly place for

children, with more child's eye vantage points and interactive graphics. And so on. But what of the year 2089?

By 2089 the National BioPark will exist within a very different Washington, D.C. My feelings about the changes in our society that will occur by then are clearly based on the prejudices that derive from my tastes and personal history. They are probably very eccentric. Nonetheless, some basic trends should be predictable. Here are some assertive predictions. I hope they are as successful as those made close to the start of this century by H. G. Wells. I think that there will be a major revolution in "urban" transportation. Personally owned autonomously controlled transportation will become incompatible with a civilized life. As a result parking lots will cease to exist at the National BioPark. There will be a movement to contain and conceal urban sprawl, to restore an uncluttered countryside. Coupled with energy-saving measures, this will produce a below-ground architecture and above-ground ruralism. The National Zoo's bermed, partly buried, education and administration building is a harbinger of this trend. A breakthrough in the biology of photosynthesis, enhanced whole-plant productivity through bioengineering, and new environmental policies will result in a great reduction of land surfaces devoted to agriculture and the restoration of original habitats throughout the United States.

All the above appearance-changing processes will have started by 2089. They will have been founded upon a new internationalism and worldwide population control. The National BioPark may be called the Smithsonian BioCenter, perhaps in a new international language. It will

have many more elements of a non-living nature than the BioPark of the year 2000. Projected holographic imagery will enable us to view the structure of animals from the skin inward, and vice versa. Comparisons between such images, simultaneous and successive, will be available on voice command. We will be able to explore the world of very small animals, large screen, Imax type, in microtheaters. And, long before 2089, we will be able to illustrate the ultimate dependency of animals on plants by building a self-contained ecosystem, a giant "Ecosphere" based on Ed Bass's innovative Biosphere II project (Maranto 1987). In this sealed system, plants and animals will coexist with no other input than sunlight. (By the year 2089 we may have eliminated dependence on plants by in vitro photosynthesis, but this will not diminish their natural importance.) At that stage meat-eaters may be able to satisfy their craving by the mass tissue culturing of muscle masses rather than animals. What an ethical issue that could provoke. Is a cultured chicken breast animate or not?

As a biologist, one of my wild dreams is that we will one day manage to recover enough hereditary material from the mummified corpse of a ground sloth or the frozen body of a mammoth to reconstruct living members of these extinct species. Certainly we should be able to find surrogate parents for a baby mammoth, but there may be no such surrogate for the ground sloth. Some extinct animals are of such intrinsic interest that their reconstruction would be a delight and not merely a seven-day wonder. Extinct birds might be even more fruitful subjects for such work; an incubator is easier to find than a surrogate womb. Perhaps the dodo could be the basis of a new resource for Third World economies.

Thomas A. Sebeok has suggested that the zoo of the future should include not just living creatures but also information processing machines such as computers and robots. This is an intriguing suggestion. If we use the BioPark to "document" the history of life on earth, including the evolution of intelligence, it clearly would be appropriate to use it to portray the development of artificial intelligence, and "animate" machines such as robots. We should start with *Robotus neanderthalensis* and perhaps by 2089 we will be able to finish with *R. sapiens.*

Enough is enough. Some of these projections probably will hit the mark. I hope so. The only current projection, by many environmentalists, that I hope fails utterly is the one that suggests that many species that exist now will continue to exist *only* in zoos!

Human and Animal Welfare

In the introductory paragraph to this essay I suggested that the last one hundred years saw an immense improvement in the human condition. This is, I believe, generally true. Despite the Holocaust, the oppression of dictators, the inhuman bombing of World War II, the atrocities committed in the "minor" wars since then, the present existence of state barbarism in many countries, terrorisms unanticipated in 1889, lingering racial and sexual discrimination, and problems of poverty and starvation, we have progressed in great strides. We have eliminated some major diseases and reduced the incidence of others to dramatic effect. Nearly all the great strides in human medicine postdate the foundation of our zoo. For the majority of humankind increased standards of hygiene and nutrition belong entirely to the

twentieth century.

We still, however, lag behind in our treatment of the other animals with which we share the earth. From this realization have grown movements for animal welfare that parallel the movements for human welfare that arose out of the conditions of Victorian society, the conditions in the developed world that are now seen mainly in the Third World. Movements for the abolition of child labor and cruelty to children, for prison reform, popular education, fair labor laws, women's rights, the ending of colonialism, against national oppressions, and for religious and political freedoms, all grew mightily at the end of the nineteenth century and peaked in the first half of our century. This century saw the Universal Declaration of Human Rights, and despite the emphasis on the rights of the aristocracy that marked the Magna Carta, emphasis on the rights of the majority only came in the eighteenth and nineteenth centuries. Thomas Paine in many ways summarized some of the rights issues that underpinned both the French and American revolutions, whatever their ultimate effects. Human rights movements are far from being unnecessary, but in many countries their mission has become less urgent, and the necessity for action less general and less widespread in society.

It seems that putting less energy into the struggle for human rights and welfare has somehow allowed us to review our relationship with the rest of the animal kingdom. Thus there has been considerable growth in the animal welfare movements and the movements of environmental concern. And now the issue of animal rights, once the preoccupation of a handful of philosophers and moralists, has become a larger concern. The Humane Society

of the United States has declared: "There is no rational basis for maintaining a moral distinction between the treatment of humans and other animals." (HSUS 1982). Of course this is not true. There are a number of perfectly rational bases for maintaining such a moral distinction; they may not be acceptable to the Humane Society, but they are rational. Clearly this is not the place to argue such a moral/ethical/philosophical matter. Suffice it to say that the issue is a vexed one. Mary Midgley (1983,61), a major philosopher-proponent of animal rights, has said: "Rights. This is a really desperate word. As any bibliography of political theory will show, it was in deep trouble long before animals were added to its worries. On the other hand it is welded more thoroughly than duty to a legal and political context. It is used descriptively for a whole network of privileges conferred by law and custom, without implying in any given case any necessary moral approval." As a biologist I have a view of our relationship with the living world that puts the whole issue in a logical context. It is perhaps more useful to explain this than to engage in philosophical controversy and ethical polemics.

We ourselves are of course animals. That realization is one of the profound results of the Darwinian revolution in biological philosophy; it extended into popular thought for a substantial number of humankind. Julian Huxley (1939) has highlighted this transformation of attitudes as follows: "Man saw himself as being set apart, with the rest of the animal kingdom created to serve his needs and pleasure. . . . In Western civilization this swing of the pendulum reached its limit in developed Christian theology and in the philosophy of Descartes: both alike inserted a qualitative and unbridgeable barrier between all men and any animals. With Darwin, the reverse swing started. Man was once again regarded as an animal, but now in the light of science rather than in unsophisticated sensibility."

Wherever we are put, with the apes or with the angels, it is true that for all of our history as a species we have killed and eaten other animals, just as all other omnivores and predators do. All life, except for autotrophic organisms, lives by eating other living things, parts thereof, or things once living. (If this is morally reprehensible, nothing escapes the opprobrium except plants that can photosynthesize and those organisms capable of complex chemosynthesis using heat as an energy source. All animals are thus condemned to "original sin.") The extent of our dependence on animal food has varied. When our ancestors emerged from the forests onto the plains, they left behind a richness and were at once confronted with a meager menu that was only extendable after the discovery of fire made cooking possible, and when grasses were cultivated to the point where they could form a stable and staple function in our diet. At the hunter-gatherer stage of our history we could not subsist as gatherers alone. In fact we hunted so efficiently that whole faunas were radically altered and large animals extinguished wherever there were plains (i.e., in Africa, Asia, Europe, and North America). Eventually it was only in the forests that hunting did not lead to great extinctions. The first animal that we domesticated, altering it first behaviorally and then physically-genetically, was the wolf that became the dog. It was as a hunting aide that we needed the dog. Its domestication precedes the domestication of herd animals.

Then in the Fertile Crescent of the Middle East (Nuclear Asia) and in Mesoamerica (Nuclear America) and elsewhere plants were cultivated and the great Neolithic Revolution started. Plants were nurtured and "unconscious selection" slowly transformed key species to meet our needs. This selection, later reinforced by the deliberate choices of agriculturists (Darwin's artificial selection), transformed the adaptations that plants had evolved for their survival into adaptations that humankind needed to use the plants for its survival. Wheat ears no longer shed their seeds; they could then be harvested with minimal loss, and so on. This step and the accompanying domestication of animals for food, work, and mobility made civilization possible. It is worth iterating this point that was so heavily emphasized by Vavilov (1926). But for our modification of the properties of other species and our consequent transformation of entire ecosystems there could be none of the things that we associate with civilization. Our very ability to speak and act about "rights" is a result of our efforts at changing nature in an absolute and radical way. If we had not exploited the muscles of horses, oxen, camels, and asses, we could not have explored or sustained populations large enough to build cities and have leisure to pursue art, philosophy, and religion. We could not have derived brain-sustaining proteins on a scale necessary to support ancient cultures without both food animals and those animals that formed living storehouses of seasonally glutted plant foods. It is ironic that the technical progress that allows us to reduce our dependence on the muscles and meat of the animal kingdom was made possible by 10,000 plus years of domestication.

We may soon finally be able to synthesize food the way the autotrophs do, from energy, carbon dioxide, and water. Then and only then will we be able to be independent of living sources of food. Then the killing will be able to stop. What we then decide will depend on the ruling morality of that age . . . morality can never outpace possibility. Will we decide that the entire world of life has to be a "peaceable kingdom" and as a result behaviorally modify carnivores so that they do not kill animals, and herbivores so that they do not kill plants? Will we decide to eliminate all phytophagus insects because they are too numerous to be reformed?

Finally, a word about freedom and animals. This is an issue that is often raised by critics of zoos. A columnist in the *Washington Post* (McCarthy 1988) wrote that caged animals in zoos "are prison inmates serving life sentences. Zoos are jails. . . ." Less extreme versions of this viewpoint are commonly held by a number of people. The implications and corollaries of this view are not obvious at first sight, but can be logically deduced. If zoos are prisons for wild animals then there must be some state for those animals that represents freedom. This is not often stated directly but the inference must surely be that this contrasting state of freedom is life in the wild, life in free nature. So we can ask are animals free in nature? My answer is that freedom is a meaningless abstraction when applied to animals in their natural ecosystems. The lessons of field biology are simple. Animals, in nature, live in a continual battle with conspecifics with whom they compete for resources like food, nest sites, shelter, mates, and so on and with other species that would prey upon them or parasitize them. Survival struggles are intense and are reflected in the prolixity of reproduction; many, many more offspring are produced than survive. Survival rates are millions to one in many fishes, thousands to one in spiders, hundreds to one in many reptiles, tens to one in birds, and closer to four to five to one in mammals. (The effect of internal development and suckling in mammals is mimicked by our nurturing of pet fishes and birds, or our propagation efforts for endangered species, resulting in great reductions in the mortalities of early life.) The intensity of the struggle to survive in free nature is also reflected in the fact that anti-predator adaptations are incredibly finely honed, testifying to the continual deadly arms race between hunters and hunted. Wild animals live short lives compared to their domestic relatives; they breed less frequently, and fewer young survive even the early stages of their infancy. For most zoo animals the results of human caring and nurturing are the same. The effects are comparable to those of civilization on our own species; our life-expectancies really only reached four score years and ten when we ceased to live "as wild animals in the freedom of nature." One could pile example upon example, incident on incident, but really what we are dealing with when this argument is raised is a Rousseau-like naivety about the innocence of the natural state. It is not and never was.

We stand at the threshold of big changes. I wish I could be here in 2089 to see the results.

Michael H. Robinson
Director
National Zoological Park
Smithsonian Institution

References

Darlington, C. D. "The Unification of Biology." *New Scientist* 13, no. 269 (1962):72–74.

HSUS. *Animal Rights.* A pamphlet published by the Humane Society of the United States, Washington, D.C., 1982.

Huxley, J. S. *Man in the Modern World.* New York: Harper, 1939.

McCarthy, C. "It's Not Fun for the Pandas." *Washington Post* (August 14, 1988), section F8.

Maranto, G. "Earth's First Visitors to Mars." *Discover* (May 1987): 27–43.

Midgley, M. *Animals and Why They Matter.* Athens: University of Georgia Press, 1983.

Vavilov, N. I. "Studies on the Origin of Cultivated Plants." *B. Applied Botany* 16 (1926): 139–248.

PICTURE CREDITS

Karl Amann
178L

Riley Caton
138

Chip Clark
2–3, 4–5, 6–7, 12, 29, 30–31, 55, 56, 57, 63, 65, 74, 79, 134, 144, 150, 192, 194

Jennifer Clark
50

Jessie Cohen, National Zoological Park
cover, 8, 10, 14, 16, 19, 20, 21, 23B, 24, 25, 34, 35, 36, 38, 42, 43, 44, 45, 46, 48, center two, 49, 51, 52, 53, 54, 58T, 60, 61, 62, 64, 66, 67, 68B, 69, 70, 73L, 76T, 77B, 78, 82, 83, 84, 85, 86, 87, 88, 89, 91, 94, 95, 96L, 100T, 104, 105, 107, 108, 109, 110, 111, 113R, 115, 118, 119, 121, 122, 123, 125, 127, 129, 132, 133, 135, 136, 137, 143, 146B, 149, 154, 155, 197

Larry Collins
112, 114T, 116

Cooper • Lecky Architects, P.C., Washington, D.C.
193T

James M. Dietz
22, 26, 32, 33, 37, 39T, 41, 157

Lou Ann Dietz
23T, 23C

Freer Gallery of Art
160

Kenneth Garrett
99, 113L

Dennis Gilbert
128

Jay Golden
140T

Craig Herndon
198

Frank Kohn
153

Library of Congress
152, 159

Laurie Marker-Kraus
140B

Office of Graphics and Exhibits, National Zoological Park
15, 17, 18, 47, 48T, 48B, 58B, 75, 77T, 92, 93, 96R, 97, 98, 100C, 100B, 101, 103T, 103B, 106, 120, 124

Olav Oftedal
80

Lori Price
114B

Miles Roberts
130–131, 139, 141, 187, 190

Kjell B. Sandved
27, 191

John Seidensticker
161, 162, 163, 164, 165, 166, 168, 169, 176T, 177B, 179, 180, 181B, 184, 185

Smithsonian Institution
193B

Smithsonian Tropical Research Institute
1 (Marcos A. Guerra), 28–29B, 39B (Carl C. Hansen)

Fiona Sunquist
170, 171, 172, 173, 174, 176B, 177T, 178R, 181T, 182, 183, 188–189

Milton H. Tierney, Jr.
59, 68T, 71, 72, 73C, 73R, 156

Amy Vedder and A. William Weber
145, 146T

Christen Wemmer
167

PUBLISHER'S ACKNOWLEDGMENTS

The Smithsonian Institution Press gratefully acknowledges the contributions of Michael H. Robinson, Robert J. Hoage, Jessie Cohen, and the staff of the Smithsonian's National Zoological Park in Washington, D.C., and its Conservation and Research Center at Front Royal, Virginia. Without their assistance, this book would not have been possible.

The editors wish to acknowledge Kjell B. Sandved, Smithsonian Institution, for his donation of the use of his photographs appearing in this book.

The editors especially thank Theresa Slowik for her efforts on behalf of this book.